INSIDER BROOKLYN

A Curated Guide to New York City's Most Stylish Borough

RACHEL FELDER

HARPER DESIGN

An Imprint of HarperCollins Publishers

For my anchor and best friend, Millie Felder,
whose much-missed namesake happily
lived and worked in—where else?—Brooklyn

Frida
the Queen o

@fishwith

Vita!

#artsinactionbushwick
#morganwalls

Contents

Introduction

If New York is the city that never sleeps, then Brooklyn is the borough that never stands still—it's always evolving, with neighborhoods that regularly reinvent themselves and a seemingly endless influx of new people and businesses that gives the area an almost tangible buzz. Over the past few years, Brooklyn has become a highly desirable place to live, eat, and shop: a chic, beguiling destination drawing in people from other neighborhoods as well as visitors from all over the world.

But navigating Brooklyn, even for New Yorkers, can be daunting. For starters, it's large—the most populated of New York City's five boroughs. Getting around isn't as immediately logical as it is in Manhattan, with its precise grid of streets. And, like many great cities, Brooklyn is comprised of neighborhoods that are distinct and sometimes a bit insular, so it's easy to feel like an intrusive outsider if you don't know exactly where to go. Not to mention the fact that some of the area's most memorable shops and restaurants are a bit hidden, tucked away on discreet little side streets or located a couple subway stops away from where most crowds tend to congregate.

This book is designed to make discovering Brooklyn and its many diverse pleasures easy and fun. Included are loads of insider favorites I've found along the way, both as a journalist who writes about fashion and travel and a local who's admittedly obsessed with knowing about where to find the most amazing gifts, fashionable clothes, and lovingly prepared and delicious cuisine.

There's a mix of brand-new openings and decades-old classics, organized by neighborhood with nearby subway stations included to take the guesswork out of figuring out where to go and how to get there. This isn't an overall guide to Brooklyn; it's a collection that's highly curated, with the full intent of offering a manageably sized but still ultravivid taste of the best of Brooklyn and its salient communities.

My own connection with Brooklyn goes back four generations, including a great-uncle who drove the trolley car that once went down Lorimer Street and a grandfather who campaigned unsuccessfully to represent his native borough in Congress. I spent many childhood weekends walking down Atlantic Avenue eating warm phyllo-covered spinach pies from Damascus Bread & Pastry (which are, incidentally, still a favorite Saturday afternoon treat) and buying bags of just-baked kasha knishes—the aroma of which is my own equivalent to Proust's madeleine—from (alas, now closed) Mrs. Stahl's in Brighton Beach. I was brought up to be proud of my roots in an era when many residents were fueled by the goal of getting out of Brooklyn; for me, the borough has always been an intoxicating magnet. As captivating as it was a few decades ago, it's exponentially more so today.

As the borough and its influence continue to expand and flourish, I hope this guide makes exploring it a straightforward, fun, and stylish experience.

PLEASE
ASK BEFORE
TAKING PHOTOS

DO NOT
TOUCH PLEASE

THINGS TO DO

BROOKLYN

CULTURAL INSTITUTIONS AND PUBLIC SPACES

Brooklyn may be just one of the five boroughs in New York City, but it has more top-notch museums, expansive parks and gardens, and performance spaces than many of the world's greatest cities. The selection included here features a mix of all of the above, but most are centrally located and all are easy to reach by subway.

BLDG 92

Brooklyn's massive Navy Yard was used by the military from 1801 through 1966; it's now the cornerstone of an increasingly vibrant emerging neighborhood. Bldg 92, the residence of Commodore Matthew Perry at the time of his opening of Japan, tracks the Yard's history through exhibits and events.

63 FLUSHING AVENUE . 11205 . A/C: HIGH ST–BROOKLYN BRIDGE; F: YORK ST;
G: CLINTON–WASHINGTON AVES . 718.907.5932 . BLDG92.ORG

BROOKLYN BOTANIC GARDEN

Founded in 1910, this fifty-two-acre urban oasis on the edge of Prospect Park is breathtaking year-round, but the annual Sakura Matsuri cherry blossom festival in the spring, when hundreds of cherry trees come gradually into bloom, is an especially breathtaking time here. The grounds also include an expansive rose garden (with more than 1,400 varieties) and the Celebrity Path, a walkway lined with stones carved with the names of famous Brooklynites like Woody Allen and Barbra Streisand.

990 WASHINGTON AVENUE . 11225 . 2/3/4/5: FRANKLIN AVE; 2/3: EASTERN PKWY–BROOKLYN MUSEUM
718.623.7200 . BBG.ORG

BROOKLYN BRIDGE PARK

This eighty-five-acre waterfront expanse on the Brooklyn side of the East River is the perfect place for taking photographs of the views of lower Manhattan and the Brooklyn and Manhattan Bridges or simply having a leisurely picnic. Numerous events are held here regularly: concerts, dance parties, and walking tours. Another highlight is Jane's Carousel, a refurbished 1922 merry-go-round that is nestled inside a transparent acrylic pavilion designed by Jean Nouvel.

BEST ENTRANCES: 1 WATER STREET/4 JORALEMON STREET . 11201
A/C: HIGH ST–BROOKLYN BRIDGE; F: YORK ST; 2/3: CLARK ST; R: COURT ST; 2/3/4/5: BOROUGH HALL
718.222.9939 . BROOKLYNBRIDGEPARK.ORG

BROOKLYN CHILDREN'S MUSEUM

The first children's museum in America, this Crown Heights institution has been inspiring kids to be more inquisitive since 1899, with events and activities as well as ongoing exhibitions.

45 BROOKLYN AVENUE . 11213 . A/C: NOSTRAND AVE; C: KINGSTON–THROOP AVES; 3: KINGSTON AVE
718.735.4400 . BROOKLYNKIDS.COM

BROOKLYN MUSEUM

On par with many of the world's top museums, the focus here is on accessible shows, often with a link to pop culture, by artists like Andy Warhol and Takashi Murakami, or to fashion, with shows on individual designers like Jean Paul Gaultier, or on a more general subject such as the art of the high heel.

200 EASTERN PARKWAY . 11238 . 2/3: EASTERN PKWY–BROOKLYN MUSEUM . 718.638.5000
BROOKLYNMUSEUM.ORG

THE CITY RELIQUARY

This idiosyncratic museum could exist only in Williamsburg. With a storefront that looks like it houses a deli or hardware store, this nonprofit, civic organization is always filled with an eclectic collection of antique items that are related to New York, like clunky glass spray seltzer bottles and paintings of baseball players from the long-defunct Brooklyn Dodgers. It also puts on rotating exhibits that evoke an era of city life that simply no longer exists, as well as holding various cultural events annually.

370 METROPOLITAN AVENUE . 11211 . G: METROPOLITAN AVE–GRAND ST; L: LORIMER ST . 718.782.4842
CITYRELIQUARY.ORG

GREEN-WOOD CEMETERY

Essentially New York City's equivalent to Paris's Père Lachaise, there are well over a half million New York City residents (as the deceased are called here) in this massive cemetery in the center of Brooklyn, including Jean-Michel Basquiat and Leonard Bernstein. In addition to tours, a variety of events are offered here throughout the year, including nighttime photography workshops and an annual concert each Memorial Day.

500 25TH STREET . 11232 . R: 25TH ST . 718.768.7300 . GREEN-WOOD.COM

NEW YORK TRANSIT MUSEUM

Centrally located down a flight of stairs in an unused subway station in Brooklyn Heights, the museum offers visitors a literal step back in time with antique trains and buses on display as well as curated exhibitions. It also frequently organizes excursions on its old subway cars to nearby destinations. Depending on the day, you may have to wait to get inside—there's sometimes a line on the sidewalk to descend from street level into the space.

BOERUM PLACE AND SCHERMERHORN STREET . 11201 . A/C/G: HOYT–SCHERMERHORN; A/C/F/R: JAY ST–
METROTECH; R: COURT ST; 2/3/4/5: BOROUGH HALL . 718.694.1600 . WEB.MTA.INFO/MTA/MUSEUM

PIONEER WORKS CENTER FOR ART AND INNOVATION

This multidisciplinary facility, founded by Brooklyn artist Dustin Yellin and housed in a 25,000-square-foot former warehouse in Red Hook, hosts exhibitions by emerging artists from around the world, as well as lectures and performances that are often a bit unconventional. It also provides workspaces for select artists, inviting the public in for monthly open studio days.

159 PIONEER STREET . 11231 . A/C/F/R: JAY ST–METROTECH; F/G: CARROLL ST . 718.596.3001
PIONEERWORKS.ORG

PROSPECT PARK

Central Park in Manhattan may well be better known, but the 585 acres that make up Brooklyn's lush Prospect Park are equally majestic. Conceived and laid out by Olmsted and Vaux, the landscape architects of Central Park, Prospect Park offers something for everyone: fields in which to play baseball, basketball, soccer, and pétanque; tennis courts and paths for bike riders; a twelve-acre zoo with an impressive menagerie; a skating rink; free concerts by major acts in the summer; and, as you'd expect from a world-class park, green expanses for strolling, picnicking, or just clearing your head.

BEST ENTRANCES: GRAND ARMY PLAZA/442 FLATBUSH AVENUE . 11238;
BARTEL-PRITCHARD SQUARE . 11215 . B/Q/S: PROSPECT PARK; F/G: 15 ST–PROSPECT PARK;
Q: PARKSIDE AVE; 2/3: EASTERN PKWY–BROOKLYN MUSEUM . 718.965.8951 . PROSPECTPARK.ORG

WEEKSVILLE HERITAGE CENTER

In the nineteenth century, Weeksville was one of the first communities of free African-Americans in America. This evocative Crown Heights museum includes several houses from that era, maintained to help visitors see how the original residents lived, and offers an inventive array of programming.

158 BUFFALO AVENUE . 11213 . A/C: UTICA AVE; 3/4: CROWN HTS–UTICA AVE . 718.756.5250
WEEKSVILLESOCIETY.ORG

LIVE MUSIC VENUES

Brooklyn has become a mecca for music lovers, from indie-rock obsessives to followers of mainstream pop superstars. For all of these fans there's a wide range of venues to see and hear their favorite artists performing live in both huge state-of-the-art theaters and small clubs. The latter are predominant in Williamsburg, where a large community of cutting-edge rock bands live and rehearse.

BABY'S ALL RIGHT

For record company talent scouts looking for the next big thing, this vibey club is a frequent haunt, especially on weeknights. As regulars, they know the food here's great, too—most notably, duck fat fries and fried chicken—as are cocktails, like the *kamakura*, an invigorating and unexpected blend of matcha tea with Maker's Mark bourbon.

146 BROADWAY . 11211 . J/M/Z: MARCY AVE . 718.599.5800 . BABYSALLRIGHT.COM

BARCLAYS CENTER

This massive and modern arena is home to two teams—basketball's Brooklyn Nets and hockey's New York Islanders—and also hosts concerts by world-renowned rock, pop, and rap artists.

620 ATLANTIC AVENUE . 11217 . B/D/N/Q/R/2/3/4/5: ATLANTIC AVE–BARCLAYS CTR . 917.618.6100
BARCLAYSCENTER.COM

THE BELL HOUSE

This former warehouse in Gowanus hosts a cross-section of up-and-coming bands, plus a hodgepodge of oddball but usually very fun events, like monthly meetings of the Secret Science Club, a geekfest focused around a lecture on a subject like neurobiology.

149 SEVENTH AVENUE . 11215 . F/G/R: 4TH AVE–9TH ST . 718.643.6510 . THEBELLHOUSENY.COM

BROOKLYN ACADEMY OF MUSIC

This cluster of venues in downtown Brooklyn, which locals simply call "BAM," is a true center for the arts, hosting music, dance, theatrical, and comedy performances by artists from around the globe; the programming, which also includes talks, films, interviews, and kid-focused options, is frequently avant-garde and always thought-provoking. At the Peter Jay Sharp Building, there's a massive opera house and movie theater, while the Harvey Theater, a couple minutes' walk away, seats nearly nine hundred. There are also a couple smaller performance spaces in the nearby Fisher Building.

30 LAFAYETTE AVENUE, 651 FULTON STREET, 321 ASHLAND PLACE . C: LAFAYETTE AVE; G: FULTON ST;
2/3/4/5: NEVINS ST . 718.636.4100 . WWW.BAM.ORG

BROOKLYN BOWL

Some might say this centrally located Williamsburg space has it all: sixteen high-tech bowling lanes, tasty food (from a kitchen overseen by the beloved New York City chain Blue Ribbon), and both live music and DJ nights.

61 WYTHE AVENUE . 11249 . G: NASSAU AVE; L: BEDFORD AVE . 718.963.3369 . BROOKLYNBOWL.COM

KINGS THEATRE

Built in 1929 as a grand cinema, this large theater recently underwent a $95 million renovation and restoration, and now hosts an eclectic lineup of artists, from the O'Jays to Jackson Browne to hipster favorites TV on the Radio.

1027 FLATBUSH AVENUE . 11226 . B/Q/2/5: CHURCH AVE; Q: BEVERLY RD . 718.856.2220 . KINGSTHEATRE.COM

MUSIC HALL OF WILLIAMSBURG

It's not fancy, but this usually packed venue is an ideal place to see alternative bands, often on tour from elsewhere in America or the United Kingdom and before they hit the big time, surrounded by a roomful of sweaty fans.

66 NORTH 6TH STREET . 11211 . L: BEDFORD AVE . 718.486.5400 . MUSICHALLOFWILLIAMSBURG.COM

ROUGH TRADE NYC

This British import is the club of choice for many of New York City's indie-rock fans since it offers clear sight lines, affordable tickets, and a constant stream of tastemaker-approved artists playing, not to mention an excellent record shop (see page 48).

64 NORTH 9TH STREET . 11249 . G: NASSAU AVE; L: BEDFORD AVE . 718.388.4111 . ROUGHTRADENYC.COM

ST. ANN'S WAREHOUSE

This concert hall has moved a few times since it was founded in a Brooklyn Heights church in 1980; now located in Dumbo, it has staged critically acclaimed performances by the likes of David Bowie, Marianne Faithfull, and Lou Reed and continues to offer a diverse—and sometimes unconventional—range of live programming.

45 WATER STREET . 11201 . F: YORK ST . 718.254.8779 . STANNSWAREHOUSE.ORG

HOTELS

Until quite recently, a Manhattan hotel seemed like the inevitable option for style-conscious visitors to New York City, since Brooklyn's choice of upscale accommodations was slim. That's rapidly changing, particularly in Williamsburg, with the opening of a handful of properties that even the most discerning traveler can appreciate.

Brooklyn Heights

1 HOTEL BROOKLYN BRIDGE

The main attractions for many guests at this new hotel are the spectacular views of the Manhattan skyline and the Statue of Liberty, but other draws include food by acclaimed New York City chef and restaurateur Seamus Mullen.

60 FURMAN STREET . 11201 . 2/3: CLARK ST . 866.615.1111 . 1HOTELS.COM/BROOKLYN_BRIDGE

Crown Heights and Bedford-Stuyvesant

THE BROOKLYN A HOTEL

Standing inside one of this boutique hotel's airy rooms—with an extra-comfy bed dressed with 300-thread-count sateen sheets and exposed brick walls decorated with commissioned photographs of Brooklyn landmarks and classic locations— guests feel like they're staying in a fancy condominium in Williamsburg. Yet this friendly property is on an active block near Nostrand Avenue, on the border of Crown Heights and Bedford-Stuyvesant, an area in the midst of an unequivocally urban mix of businesses and residences that's becoming more gentrified.

1199 ATLANTIC AVENUE . 11216 . A/C: NOSTRAND AVE . 718.789.1500 . THEBROOKLYNNY.COM

Gowanus

GOWANUS INN & YARD

Matthew Abramcyk, a hipster restaurateur who has worked on hot spots like Beatrice Inn and Super Linda, is the boldface name behind this seventy-nine-room newcomer to Brooklyn's hotel scene. The see-and-be-seen atmosphere is a key part of its appeal as are the inventive food and cocktails in the hotel's restaurant.

645–651 UNION STREET . 11215 . B/D/N/R/Q/2/3/4/5: ATLANTIC AVE–BARCLAYS CTR; R: UNION ST
INFO@GOWANUSINN.COM

Greenpoint

THE BOX HOUSE HOTEL

This boutique property, located in a decidedly untouristy part of Greenpoint, has large rooms, with mini kitchens and hardwood floors that make guests feel like local residents.

77 BOX STREET . 11222 . G: GREENPOINT AVE; 7: VERNON BLVD–JACKSON AVE . 718.383.3800
THEBOXHOUSEHOTEL.COM

Williamsburg

McCARREN HOTEL & POOL

This well-located midsize hotel offers surprisingly upscale amenities in its sixty-four rooms—like Frette sheets, Davines shampoo and conditioner—and is particularly popular in the summer for one key reason: the saltwater pool, one of the largest in New York City, with its massive deck for sunning.

160 NORTH 12TH STREET . 11249 . G: NASSAU AVE; L: BEDFORD AVE . 718.218.7500
CHELSEAHOTELS.COM/US/BROOKLYN/MCCARREN-HOTEL-AND-POOL/ABOUT

URBAN COWBOY

Consider this hotel Williamsburg by way of Wyoming: a wood-covered lodge on a quiet Brooklyn street with an airy bed-and-breakfast inside. The property's focal point is a large ground-floor living room where guests tend to mingle, relax, and linger over coffee and pastries from local purveyors.

111 POWERS STREET . 11211 . G: METROPOLITAN AVE; L: LORIMER ST . 347.840.0525
URBANCOWBOYBNB.COM

THE WILLIAM VALE

If you want a room with a view, the William Vale might just be for you, as the accommodations at this large Williamsburg property were designed with floor-to-ceiling windows and balconies to maximize clear sighting of the East River and both Brooklyn and Manhattan.

55 WYTHE AVENUE . 11229 . G: NASSAU AVE; L: BEDFORD AVE . 718.631.8400 . THEWILLIAMVALE.COM

THE WILLIAMSBURG HOTEL

This industrial-looking 150-room hotel, overseen by a team that has worked at chicster Manhattan properties like the Gramercy Park Hotel and the Jane, includes a massive ballroom for weddings and events, a rooftop pool, a lower-level nightclub, and three bars for ample imbibing options.

96 WYTHE AVENUE . 11229 . G: NASSAU AVE; L: BEDFORD AVE . 718.362.8100
THEWILLIAMSBURGHOTEL.COM

WYTHE HOTEL

This vibrant hotel is a mainstay of the Williamsburg scene, complete with a foodie-approved restaurant, Reynard. There's also a rooftop bar, the Ides, which offers magnificent views of the Manhattan skyline. Expect a long wait for a seat there, particularly on weekends; tables aren't reservable in advance, except for large parties.

80 WYTHE AVENUE . 11229 . G: NASSAU AVE; L: BEDFORD AVE . 718.460.8000 . WYTHEHOTEL.COM

CULINARY MAINSTAYS

Like many places these days, Brooklyn has a flourishing culinary scene with new restaurants, young chefs, and imaginative dishes. Great food, however, is nothing new in the borough, which has been a compelling destination for gourmands for many years. Lots of its establishments aren't fancy or refined, but they're absolutely worth the pilgrimage for dishes that have become institutions unto themselves.

BROOKLYN ICE CREAM FACTORY

Located in a converted 1922 fireboat house on the Fulton Ferry Landing Pier in Dumbo, this ice cream shop has two key draws: one of the most spectacular vistas of New York City (the Brooklyn Bridge, Manhattan skyline, and Statue of Liberty are in full view) and, of course, the handful of small-batch ice cream flavors made on the premises, mostly in classic varieties like vanilla, chocolate, and—arguably most delicious—coffee. There is a second location in Greenpoint at 97 Commercial Street.

1 WATER STREET . 11201 . A/C: HIGH ST–BROOKLYN BRIDGE . 718.246.3963
BROOKLYNICECREAMFACTORY.COM

DI FARA PIZZA

For a slice of classic New York City pizza—folded in half and eaten with one hand, the local way—devotees have been coming to this unassuming Midwood spot, which many fans consider to be the city's best, since the 1960s. Although the pizza is delicious on its own, you can top their slices with a choice of high-quality, authentic toppings, including porcini mushrooms, broccoli rabe, and sun-dried roasted peppers.

1424 AVENUE J . 11230 . Q: AVENUE J . 718.258.1367 . DIFARA.COM

FORTUNATO BROTHERS

Open since 1976, this much-loved Williamsburg bakery harks back to an era when the neighborhood was filled with more Italian families than hipsters. It still serves the authentic pastries, gelato, and excellent espresso that it has offered for decades.

289 MANHATTAN AVENUE . 11211 . G: METROPOLITAN AVE; L: LORIMER ST . 718.387.2281
FORTUNATOBROTHERS.COM

GRIMALDI'S COAL BRICK-OVEN PIZZERIA

Two things never change at Grimaldi's: there are no slices (in other words, you have to order whole pies only) and there's always a line. The faithful clientele doesn't mind the wait, as the pizza is otherworldly, baked in a coal-fired brick oven that imbues each pie with a hint of earthy toastiness. Grimaldi's makes every ingredient by hand, as it has for generations, including the mozzarella—the most delectably gooey, velvety detail on each pie.

1 FRONT STREET . 11201 . A/C: HIGH ST–BROOKLYN BRIDGE; F:YORK ST . 718.858.4300 . GRIMALDIS-PIZZA.COM

NATHAN'S FAMOUS

Nathan's delicious, deep red, mustard-schmeared hot dogs have been virtually synonymous with Coney Island since 1916, and thousands come here to observe the annual hot dog–eating contest—which awards a male and female champion— on Independence Day every year. Dining here is a boisterous event, particularly on a warm, weekend day, but worth the genuine Brooklyn experience, along with a stroll on the boardwalk and a visit to the amusement park nearby.

1310 SURF AVENUE . 11224 . D/F/N/Q: CONEY ISLAND–STILLWELL AVE . 718.333.2202
NATHANSFAMOUS.COM

PETER LUGER STEAKHOUSE

This iconic Williamsburg restaurant, which opened in 1887, has been popular long before the neighborhood became desirable or hip. A diverse crowd flocks here for perfectly aged and charred cuts of meat, but there are other impressive— if traditional—offerings on the menu, like gargantuan shrimp cocktail and rich creamed spinach. Cash only.

78 BROADWAY . 11211 . J/M/Z: MARCY AVE . 718.387.7400 . PETERLUGER.COM

THE RIVER CAFÉ

New Yorkers have come to this award-winning restaurant, nestled under the Brooklyn Bridge, for marriage proposals and anniversaries since it opened in 1977. It has a very romantic ambiance, plus a truly exceptional view of the Manhattan skyline. The classic New American cuisine is also excellent, as is the wine list, which is renowned above all for its reds.

1 WATER STREET . 11201 . A/C: HIGH ST–BROOKLYN BRIDGE; 2/3: CLARK ST . 718.522.5200
THERIVERCAFE.COM

SAHADI'S

This enticing store has been a hub for mouthwatering and often hard-to-find delicacies for many decades. The standouts are Middle Eastern treats—since the Sahadi family, which still owns the business after one hundred years, originally came from Lebanon—like succulent olives, extra-creamy hummus, and hot sauces and teas. Also not to miss: the excellent homemade prepared food offered deli-style in back, including hearty flatbread smeared with Arabic spices.

187 ATLANTIC AVENUE . 11201 . 2/3/4/5: BOROUGH HALL . 718.624.4550 . SAHADIFINEFOODS.COM

FLEA MARKETS

On weekends in Brooklyn, both tourists and New Yorkers flock to something that's colorful, eclectic, and free: one of the borough's effulgent flea markets, held year-round and brimming with collectibles, crafts, artisanal edibles, and oddball trinkets that many locals refer to as tchotchkes, the Yiddish word for "knickknacks." Even if you're not in the mood to shop, these markets guarantee great people watching in a lively environment.

ARTISTS AND FLEAS

Every Saturday and Sunday, more than one hundred vendors cram into this market's large indoor space, where hand-designed jewelry, nifty smartphone cases, clothing from the 1960s and 1970s, and homegrown beauty lines are all for sale.

70 NORTH 7TH STREET . 11249 . L: BEDFORD AVE . 917.488.4203 . ARTISTSANDFLEAS.COM

BROOKLYN FLEA

This colorful set of flea markets is a Brooklyn institution despite the fact that it was launched only in 2008. During warm and warmish months—namely, April through early autumn—the Flea is headquartered in large outdoor spaces in Fort Greene on Saturdays and in Williamsburg on Sundays, plus a smaller spot in Park Slope on both days. During the colder months, it relocates indoors to a location that changes each year. Expect to find antiques, handmade gifts, food, and, usually, crowds of shoppers from around the world.

SATURDAYS: 176 LAFAYETTE AVENUE . 11238 . C: LAFAYETTE AVE; G: CLINTON–WASHINGTON AVES
SUNDAYS: 50 KENT AVENUE . 11249 . G: NASSAU AVE; L: BEDFORD AVE
BROOKLYNFLEA.COM

BUSHWICK FLEA MARKET

A newcomer to the outdoor market scene, this manageably sized lot, open Saturdays and Sundays, is a place to find vintage bargains, particularly women's clothing.

CORNER OF WYCKOFF AND WILLOUGHBY . L: JEFFERSON AVE . BWFLEA.COM

SMORGASBURG

Smorgasburg is an outdoor culinary flea market with distinctive local purveyors selling eat-on-the-spot food and drinks. Organized by the founders of the Brooklyn Flea, it's open April through mid-autumn in Williamsburg—where it started—and is situated in the center of verdant Prospect Park.

SATURDAYS: 90 KENT AVENUE . 11211 . G: NASSAU AVE; L: BEDFORD AVE
SUNDAYS: BREEZE HILL, PROSPECT PARK . 11225 . B/Q/S: PROSPECT PARK; F/G: 15TH ST–PROSPECT PARK
SMORGASBURG.COM

THE NEIGHBORHOODS

Williamsburg

For many decades, Williamsburg was a community distinguished by large factories—like the Domino Sugar Refinery, which opened in 1882—and a population made up mostly of immigrants from Eastern Europe, Italy, and, beginning in the 1960s, Puerto Rico. Over the last ten to fifteen years, the neighborhood has changed enormously, with numerous manufacturing plants transformed into high-end housing and many immigrants priced out of living in the area, although some remain, including a large group of ultra-orthodox Hasidic Jews that are based in the southern part of the area. For many visitors and locals alike, Williamsburg has come to epitomize modern Brooklyn—a community characterized by a variety of unusual stores, restaurants serving imaginative food, and a population of vibrant, culturally minded, and latte-loving young residents. Easy access to and from Manhattan makes the neighborhood an ideal area to explore, even if some folks complain about the vast amount of development over the past decade or so. The streets surrounding the Bedford Avenue subway station can get congested with locals and visitors, especially on weekends, but that's an added incentive to discover some of the more under-the-radar spots located deeper within the community.

Catbird

This appealing boutique and its jewelry, all designed in-house, hits a few shopping sweet spots: everything has a touch of both wholesomeness and edge, nothing's too trendy but it all still feels in style, and prices are low enough that even multiple impulse purchases can be made guilt-free. No wonder it's as popular with locals as it is with visitors, who pack the store on weekends. If you're not in the mood for jewelry, there's also a small but well-chosen selection of like-minded items—Formulary 55 bath products, letterpress greeting cards—that make it hard to leave without buying something. Although most things here are on the wear-everyday casual side, there's also a Catbird Wedding Annex a few blocks away at 540 Driggs Avenue, offering rings to celebrate marriages, engagements, and other commitments.

219 BEDFORD AVENUE . 11211   L: BEDFORD AVE   ☎ 718.599.3457
🌐 CATBIRDNYC.COM

Okonomi

In a sense, this tiny, authentically Japanese spot is three restaurants in one. During the day, there's just one offering: traditional Ichiju Sansai Japanese breakfast, consisting of grilled fish, steamed rice, and sharp pickled vegetables with the optional plop of sea urchin and/or a soft-poached egg. The admittedly hearty combination brings in a steady flow of morning customers, although it is served through lunchtime. Weeknights, the menu is ramen-based, shaking up predictable bowls of steaming noodles with the addition of ingredients like bacon and eggs. On Saturday and Sunday evenings, there's a single seating at 8 P.M. and a special seafood-centric omakase meal served. Those two nights get booked up about a month in advance; otherwise, there's usually a wait for a table—there are, after all, just twelve seats; most guests spend that time having a perfectly pulled espresso—or a quick trim—next door at Blind Barber, a barbershop with a café.

150 AINSLIE STREET . 11211 🚇 G: METROPOLITAN AVE; L: LORIMER ST ☎ 646.262.1358
🌐 OKONOMIBK.COM

Hickoree's Floor Two

Hickoree's is not the best-known guys' store in Brooklyn—due in large part to the inconspicuous location, behind a slim door and up a flight of stairs in a small building near the Williamsburg Bridge—but it's one of the most reliable, offering stylish essentials, mainly with a vintage feel. Most of the pieces here have a touch of utilitarianism about them, like dark-and-stiff Kaptain Sunshine Japanese denim jeans and hefty cobalt blue Vetra twill jackets, made in France and reminiscent of the trademark garment of legendary *New York Times* street photographer Bill Cunningham. There is also an array of non-clothing items—gridded notebooks, rugged Phigvel leather key holders, canvas totes, and, to tap in to every man's inner boy, Buckthorn branch slingshots—that have been chosen with an expert eye.

109 SOUTH 6TH STREET, SECOND FLOOR . 11211 🚇 J/M/Z MARCY AVE; L: BEDFORD AVE
☎ 347.294.0005 ⊕ HICKOREES.COM

FLOOR
TWO

SHOP CLASS

NORTH MANUAL   VOCATIONAL

DROPOUT

TAFT MODEL # TF-03

Fuego 718

It's easy to forget you're in South Williamsburg when you step into Fuego 718, which feels a lot like a Mexico City street market a couple days before each autumn's festivities for the Day of the Dead, or alternately, in some of its nooks, the Frida Kahlo section of a museum gift shop. The large store is filled with loads of miniature skeletons (although, really, the vibe is jolly with a bit of kitsch as opposed to dark and macabre) plus colorful little trinkets from Peru and Haiti as well as, of course, Mexico. There are also paper-bound notebooks, pillows, and other small home decorations, and smile-inducing greeting cards by My Zoetrope. Nothing's particularly expensive, so the store is popular for impromptu gifts.

249 GRAND STREET . 11211 👑 G: METROPOLITAN AVE; J/M/Z: MARCY AVE ☎ 718.302.2913
🌐 FUEGO718.COM

Space Ninety 8

Although this multilevel hyperstore is part of the Urban Outfitters chain, it feels undeniably unique, cool, and part of the neighborhood. Locally made clothes—including home items, accessories, and beautifiers—are spotlighted and updated regularly to cycle in a variety of designers and resonate seasonally. The store also frequently showcases little-known brands and carries a selection of vintage clothes, as well as trend-embracing new pieces for men and women, plus footwear; in the basement is a record shop with loads of vinyl and a handful of guitars for an impromptu shopping-inspired jam. Upstairs is Esh, a bar and restaurant helmed by *Top Chef* winner Ilan Hall. The focus, along with people watching, is on grilled dishes with an Israeli spin, like tender, toothsome octopus prepared with Middle Eastern spices.

98 NORTH 6TH STREET . 11249 🚇 G: METROPOLITAN AVE; L: BEDFORD AVE ☎ 718.599.0209
🌐 SPACENINETY8.COM

Bedford Cheese Shop

As the name implies, the specialty here is cheese, curated from small New York State purveyors as well as generations-old, family-run farms in Europe. The store is a seamless fit in a neighborhood that's filled with foodies, especially on weekends, when the Smorgasburg culinary flea market is held just a few blocks away. But there's much more in this jam-packed store, which stocks pantry items like mustards and cookies that are ideal for gifts, even if those purchases entail a plane ride home. There's a deep selection of local brands like Empire Mayonnaise, FINE & RAW Chocolate, and the excellent, quirky-flavored line Anarchy in a Jar, but there are also imports from Italy, France, Great Britain, and beyond. If the selection seems overwhelming, the knowledgeable staff is always there to help.

229 BEDFORD AVENUE . 11211 ☗ L: BEDFORD AVE ☎ 718.599.7588

🌐 BEDFORDCHEESESHOP.COM

Beam

On a sunny day, with light streaming into the store through large windows, it's hard to imagine a more enticing home store than Beam, which offers a large selection of items that are polished without taking themselves too seriously. But while there's certainly a touch of cheekiness to some of the goods it offers—pillows reading "merde" and "go to the gym," a corkscrew shaped like a house key, a plastic breakfast-in-bed tray printed with an image of bacon and eggs—ultimately it's simply a great source of creative home items and gifts that you won't find everywhere. On the more serious side, Beam sells pillows, rugs, and a bit of furniture, but most of the loyal clientele come here for the smaller items as well as a little design inspiration.

240 KENT AVENUE . 11249 🚇 G: METROPOLITAN AVE; L: BEDFORD AVE ☎ 646.450.1469
🌐 BEAMBK.COM

Nora Kogan

Equal parts precious and punk rock, most of Nora Kogan's jewelry isn't for wallflowers. (Wearing pieces like the "Boob Ring"—a finger-surrounding set of breasts precisely enameled over sterling silver or cast in 18-karat rose gold with pavé diamond nipples—promises to be a conversation starter.) Yet somehow her statement pieces are beautiful as well as brash, toned down by their precious materials and irrefutable artistry. Some make more classic statements, like a revolving collection of unique engagement rings built around deeply colored stones (like emeralds) that offer a more subtle but equally eye-catching twist on the expected.

103 METROPOLITAN AVENUE . 11249   G: METROPOLITAN AVE; L: BEDFORD AVE   ☎ 718.398.4459
🌐 NORAKOGAN.COM

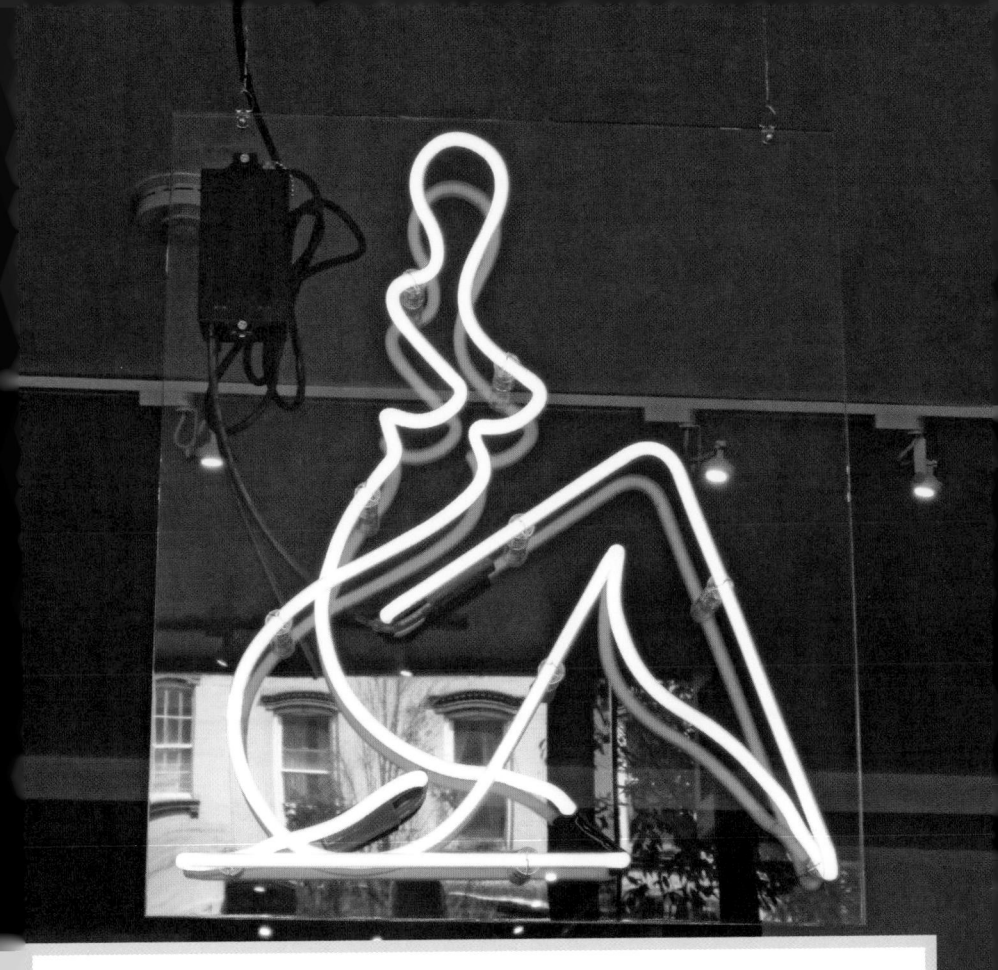

Narcisse NYC

In a particularly approachable way, this female-focused boutique carries everything for the boudoir for a diverse customer base: hipsters, brides-to-be, condo-dwelling execs, and even some of the neighborhood's religious Jewish women shop here for underpinnings. Narcisse sells mostly lingerie: beautiful bras and panties from brands like Agent Provocateur, Marlies Dekkers, and Hanky Panky, often in bright colors and lace, although some of what's here is more reminiscent of *Fifty Shades of Grey*, like silk restraints, masks, and battery-operated adult-only bedroom toys. Everything is displayed tastefully and accessibly, and the gently amicable staff makes even bashful customers at ease.

110 NORTH 6TH STREET . 11249 🚇 L: BEDFORD AVE ☎ 718.302.1760
🌐 NARCISSENYC.COM

Bird

Bird was a pioneer of Brooklyn shopping: its original location, on 7th Avenue in Park Slope, was one of the first designer clothing boutiques to have a true SoHo vibe instead of another small-time enterprise on a residential block. The store's Williamsburg location is its largest: 2,500 square feet of LEED-certified retail space, including men's and women's clothing and accessories. The selection here is on the polished casual side: French A.P.C. separates, dresses by Rachel Comey, men's relaxed oxfords by RTH, and Isabel Marant Étoile, sturdy workbags by the fashion-editor-beloved Canadian brand Want Les Essentiels de la Vie. Unlike Bird's other locations in the heart of Cobble Hill and the Park Slope original, there is a smattering of higher-end designer pieces, too, like Marni dresses and separates by Dries Van Noten. A few times a year, the shop rotates the bright art on the walls, replacing it with new pieces by mostly local artists.

203 GRAND STREET . 11211   G: METROPOLITAN AVE; L: BEDFORD AVE   ☎ 718.388.1655
🌐 SHOPBIRD.COM

Berlyn65

In her sunny jewel box of a boutique, stylist Serap Bahadir sells colorful items that have caught her eye: chunky statement necklaces to liven up plain white tank tops, multicolored bangles to wear in a stack, and softly tinted Turkish towels in various sizes to drape over a sofa or bathroom rail. There's a sense of discovery about the store (the entrance to which, incidentally, is through a door inside an adjacent restaurant) and a touch of worldly hippie to Bahadir's aesthetic, both personally and in the merchandise she carries. Offering both bold and subtle items, the selection makes Berlyn65 a reliable source of unique gifts, even if you end up keeping them for yourself.

346 BEDFORD AVENUE . 11211 🚇 J/M/R TO MARCY AVE; L: BEDFORD AVE ☎ 917.338.7570
🌐 BERLYN65.COM

Idol Brooklyn

In a sense, Idol Brooklyn offers the clothing equivalent of Williamsburg: pieces with street-smart attitude, style, a touch of the unexpected, and prices that are a lot higher than what you might expect to find outside of Manhattan. Sold here is a well-selected array of men's high-fashion clothes from the sort of designers (like Rick Owens, Yohji Yamamoto, and Haider Ackermann) that take a healthy dose of confidence to pull off, with some more wearable pieces such as logo tees by tastemaker Japanese brands like Human Made that will appeal to the less adventurous. Despite all the expensive labels and black clothing, the shopping experience at Idol is decidedly unintimidating, thanks in large part to its buoyant, approachable staff.

101 METROPOLITAN AVENUE . 11249 🚇 G: METROPOLITAN AVE; L: BEDFORD AVE ☎ 718.599.4365
🌐 IDOLBROOKLYN.COM

Xixa

There's nothing predictable about the Mexican-meets-Asian menu at this well-liked dinner spot in South Williamsburg, owned by the husband-and-wife team that also own Traif, a similarly popular restaurant nearby. (The name Xixa is pronounced shiksa, Yiddish for "a girl who's not Jewish," in honor of chef Jason Markus's shiksa wife.) Combinations you wouldn't think would work—like árbol-chile-covered edamame, Thai-spiced guacamole—simply do, with the food leaning toward the spicy side. To wash it all down is a selection of housemade, originally flavored aguas frescas (like tomatillo limeade) that can be mixed with tequila, although the wine list—divided, instead of by region, by intensity, each of which is rather hilariously named after a quirky roster of celebrities including Elizabeth Taylor, Courtney Love, and Liberace—is also strong.

241 SOUTH 4TH STREET . 11211 🚇 J/M/Z: MARCY AVE ☎ 718.388.8860
🌐 XIXANY.COM

Fellow Barber

At most guycentric barbershops, the waiting area might well consist of a couple sticky, vinyl-covered chairs near the door. Not at this branch of Fellow Barber, where a sixteen-foot curved wood bench in the middle of the floor beckons clients to sit, relax, and maybe grab a cappuccino from the barista at Grade Coffee, located inside. For those not opting for a trim or shave in one of its nine Belmont barber's chairs from the 1960s, Fellow Barber offers products for sale from brands like Malin + Goetz, D. R. Harris, Alder, and others, as well as its own line of products.

101 NORTH 8TH STREET . 11249　🚇 L: BEDFORD AVE　☎ 718.522.4959
🌐 FELLOWBARBER.COM

Treatment by Lanshin

While it focuses mostly on alternative health treatments like acupuncture and cupping, this warm and approachable storefront feels neither antiseptically medical nor New Age-y. The clientele is diverse—artists, editors, lawyers, and Wall Street executives, some of whom travel here from Manhattan—as is the menu of services, which also includes intensive facials (for issues like acne as opposed to, say, anti-aging) and Ortho-Bionomy, a type of osteopathic massage. For many people in the neighborhood, it's simply a friendly place to come in and pick up feel-good products (face oil from Laurel Whole Plant Organics, Fig & Yarrow body scrub, probiotics, and cod liver oil) while soaking in the good homey vibes.

129 ROEBLING STREET . 11211 🚇 G: METROPOLITAN AVE; L: BEDFORD AVE ☎ 718.388.4788
🌐 LANSHIN.COM

BAGGU

BAGGU's popular collection launched in 2007 with a handy item that's hard not to appreciate: a light, sturdy, capacious tote bag, offered in a variety of colors, designed to easily fold into a purse or pocket, and cheap enough to buy in multiples. That first design now comes in a large selection of patterns and colors; it's also available in leather as well as the nylon original. The line also includes subsequent creations, like canvas rucksacks, extra-roomy weekend bags, and smaller items like key chains and change purses. The shop is busy pretty much all the time, appealing to both locals needing a carryall for groceries and visitors in need of an extra bag to get a vacation's worth of purchases back home.

242 WYTHE AVENUE . 11249 🚇 L: BEDFORD AVE ☎ 800.605.0759
🌐 BAGGU.COM

Lilia

A new establishment but already a foodie magnet, Lilia is the creation of Michelin-starred chef Missy Robbins, formerly of Manhattan's A Voce and Chicago's Spiaggia, and restaurateur Matt Kliegman, whose hand is in Manhattan cool-kid spots like the Smile and Black Seed Bagels. Although the food is as serious and as seriously delicious as you'd expect, the vibe is commensurately casual with this calm Williamsburg corner, which formerly housed a car repair shop. Fresh handmade pasta, a Robbins specialty, is one of the best things to order here, but there's also meat and fish seared on a wood-burning grill, plus a small takeout area with surprisingly hearty baked goods to eat on the go.

567 UNION AVENUE . 11211 🚇 G: METROPOLITAN AVE; L: LORIMER ST ☎ 718.576.3095
🌐 LILIANEWYORK.COM

Saved

There are many excellent tattoo parlors in Brooklyn these days, especially in Williamsburg and Greenpoint, but the general consensus among aficionados is that Saved is the best. Naturally, that boils down to the precise skills of its artists. Standouts on the team include co-owners Scott Campbell—whose clients have included fashion designer Marc Jacobs and actors like Heath Ledger and Orlando Bloom—and Stephanie Tamez, who specializes in painterly large-scale tattoos. Saved's popularity means it's best to make an advance appointment but, like most tattoo spots, they do accept walk-ins.

426 UNION AVENUE . 11211 🚇 G: METROPOLITAN AVE; L: LORIMER ST ☎ 718.486.0850
🌐 SAVEDTATTOO.COM

Rough Trade NYC

Even in the age of downloads and file sharing, every cool neighborhood deserves a great record shop. In Williamsburg, that store is British import Rough Trade. There are copious amounts of vinyl here, particularly of releases by independent and critically acclaimed (but sometimes niche in appeal) artists. Nonetheless, the scope of music is vast and includes quite a few musical genres. The staff is encyclopedic but never elitist, so it's easy to get suggestions if you want them; they might also point you toward a book on sex, drugs, or rock 'n' roll: there's a large selection on the mezzanine. There's also a Ping-Pong table, a photo booth, and a compact outpost of the popular Greenpoint café Five Leaves for a latte or hearty beef and ale pie; the store even has its own (excellent) nightclub that presents gigs by touring rock bands, mostly in the alternative vein.

64 NORTH 9TH STREET . 11249 🚇 G: NASSAU AVE; L: BEDFORD AVE ☎ 718.388.4111
🌐 ROUGHTRADENYC.COM

Marlow & Sons

The owner of this evocative restaurant and takeout spot, Andrew Tarlow, is frequently credited with setting Williamsburg's still-snowballing culinary scene in motion when he opened Diner, his first foodie-beloved establishment, in a metal Kullman dining car from the 1920s in 1998. He's now got a mini-empire (including the Wythe Hotel and a large handful of restaurants), but Marlow & Sons arguably remains the snug jewel in the company's crown, offering essentially gourmet comfort food—egg sandwiches and frittatas in the morning; oysters from nearby and authentic Spanish-style potato tortillas later in the day—to a steady stream of locals and gourmands making a special trip.

81 BROADWAY . 11249 🚆 J/M/Z: MARCY AVE ☎ 718.384.1441
🌐 MARLOWANDSONS.COM

Marlow Goods

This librarylike space on the ground floor of the Wythe Hotel is at its core a gift shop—where you'll sometimes find guests precariously perched on their wheelie bags, sending emails as they're checking out. But the Wythe's interpretation of this hospitality mainstay translates into a selection of books, gifts, and baseball caps and tees that's aimed at neighbors as much as visitors. Standouts include the store's own line of quietly stylish handbags and small leather goods designed by Kate Huling and crafted from extra-soft cowskin.

80 WYTHE AVENUE . 11249 🚇 G: NASSAU AVE; L: BEDFORD AVE ☎ 718.384.1441
🌐 MARLOWGOODS.COM

The Kinfolk Store

Kinfolk is a very Williamsburgian hyphenated hybrid—shop-café-bar-studio-gallery-nightspot with DJs and performances—that makes complete sense combined into two spaces on a busy stretch of Wythe Avenue. During the day, it's decidedly relaxed—with locals sitting with laptops eating avocado toast with feta, dill, and mint, and a roasted vegetable salad; shoppers picking up highbrow magazines; nifty pens imported from Germany and Japan; and logo baseball caps. At night things get a bit more lively, with crowds staying late and enjoying creative cocktails like the "Next of Kin," with Aquavit and kombucha. The shop's merchandise leans toward guys—for which Kinfolk designs clothing, offered alongside other brands—but attracts plenty of female customers as well.

90 AND 94 WYTHE AVENUE . 11249 🚇 G: NASSAU AVE; L: BEDFORD AVE ☎ 347.689.4939
🌐 KINFOLKLIFE.COM

Rose Red & Lavender

Located on a plain, mostly residential, relatively ungentrified Williamsburg block, florist Rose Red & Lavender is an oasis of lush, countrified calm with a hint of neighborhood-appropriate spunk. There are the obligatory vivid flowers and plants, but they are displayed among a smattering of old ceramic bookends and curios, giving the space a funky, homespun appeal. A specialty here is arrangements for backyard and apartment terrace gardens, even if they are, as is so often the case in New York City, very tiny; the store will help landscape and maintain the gardens, if needed, too. The shop also regularly offers classes on flower arranging and other floral-related crafts, in addition to selling a small but top-notch selection of cards and little gifts.

653 METROPOLITAN AVENUE . 11211   G: METROPOLITAN AVE; L: LORIMER ST   ☎ 718.486.3569
🌐 ROSEREDANDLAVENDER.COM

Heatonist

The name of this mostly unadorned store is a play on words that refers to the sole item it sells: hot sauce. Even so, there's no shortage of choices here: the selection includes up to 150 varieties at any given time, from Moroccan style harissa to more fluid condiments with a Thai or Mexican slant. One favorite is the sinus-clearing Quetzalcoatl Ghost Chile Hot Sauce, redolent of brown sugar and cumin as well as heat. The store is the brainchild of hot sauce–obsessed entrepreneur Noah Chaimberg, who raised money on Kickstarter to open it and has put together a small team of "sommeliers" to advise shoppers on what to buy, encouraging tasting along the way at a wooden sample bar near the entrance.

121 WYTHE AVENUE . 11249   🚇 G: NASSAU AVE; L: BEDFORD AVE   ☎ 718.599.0838
🌐 HEATONIST.COM

Mast Brothers Chocolate

Brooklyn has become a foodie mecca over the last decade or so, with connoisseur chocolatiers like Jacques Torres, FINE & RAW, and Nunu helping lead the way. For many gourmands, Mast Brothers is the brand that's become immutably linked with the borough's artisanally produced chocolate scene. Its large bars are sourced from top-tier beans from Peru, Belize, and Papua New Guinea, and blended with ingredients like coffee from Stumptown Coffee Roasters and black truffles. The chocolate is made at this lively facility, which offers factory tours and sells bars on a long table up front. A couple doors down (at 105 A), there's a Mast-run café with drinking chocolate—available hot or cold—and pastries.

111 NORTH 3RD STREET . 11211 ⚲ G: METROPOLITAN AVE; L: BEDFORD AVE ☎ 718.388.2625
🌐 MASTBROTHERS.COM

LÁSZLÓ MOHOLY-NAGY

PREST

Alex Katz New York

Irish Museum of Modern Art

GARMENTS FOR GOOD
crewcuts

B BAU

DONALD

J.Crew

With sun streaming in through skylights and rough-hewn thick wooden beams on the high ceilings, it's easy to forget that this large space, bifurcated into men's and women's sections, is a branch of national retailer J.Crew. But that it is, with the mix of wearable staples-with-a-twist you'd expect, displayed in a way that feels a touch more trendy than in some other locations. Included is a compact section dedicated to childrenswear from the brand's crewcuts line.

234 WYTHE AVENUE . 11249 🚇 L: BEDFORD AVE ☎ 718.384.3027
🌐 STORES.JCREW.COM/WYTHE-AVE

Mociun

There's an impressive breadth of items in Mociun's compact, luminous space: colorful, frizzled yarn rugs, earthy white pottery mugs, brightly colored bowls, and the category that is its trademark: jewelry, with a priority on pieces that are unpredictable but actually quite easy to wear and graceful, like rings that pair chunky turquoise with diamonds in a way that's equally earthy and refined. The store's founder, Caitlin Mociun, designs some of the work. She also carries other lines and some vintage items; standouts include the myriad of stud earring styles, many adorned with pinprick diamonds and sold either singly to wear mismatched or as more traditional pairs.

224 WYTHE AVENUE . 11249 🚇 G: METROPOLITAN AVE; L: BEDFORD AVE ☎ 718.387.3731
🌐 MOCIUN.COM

CAFFEINE FIXES

Decades ago, Brooklyn was sometimes called the "borough of churches," thanks to its many houses of worship. These days, Williamsburg could be accurately known as the neighborhood of coffeehouses. Here are some of the most essential spots for latte lovers.

BLIND BARBER

This community-magnet café, with an adjacent barbershop, is equal parts those at work on laptops and folks getting together. In addition to excellent coffee, there's light food and beer on tap.

524 LORIMER STREET . 11211   G: METROPOLITAN AVE; L: LORIMER ST   ☎ 718.599.2435
⊕ BLINDBARBER.COM

BLUE BOTTLE COFFEE

The best time to stop by this lofty spot is in the summertime, when the wall-size front window is raised open and customers also take their cold-drip iced-coffee on the bench outside.

160 BERRY STREET . 11249   L: BEDFORD AVE   ☎ 718.387.4160   ⊕ BLUEBOTTLECOFFEE.COM

GIMME COFFEE!

Both locations of this neighborhood mainstay attract a steady stream of customers all day for no-nonsense espressos and cappuccinos, complete with lovely patterns in the frothy foam.

495 LORIMER STREET; 107 ROEBLING STREET . 11211   L: LORIMER ST; L: BEDFORD AVE
☎ 718.388.7771; 718.388.4595   ⊕ GIMMECOFFEE.COM

MATCHABAR

The specialty at this slender café is, as the name suggests, fine-powdered Japanese matcha tea, used deliciously in matchaccinos, lattes, and even muffins and other baked snacks.

93 WYTHE AVENUE . 11249   G: NASSAU AVE; L: BEDFORD AVE   ☎ 718.599.0015
⊕ MATCHABARNYC.COM

OSLO COFFEE ROASTERS

Oslo is fussy about its beans—all sourced from small, artisanal roasters—but that's the only thing that's fussy about this pair of down-to-earth neighborhood coffeehouses, each a regular morning stop for many locals.

133 ROEBLING STREET AND 328 BEDFORD AVENUE . 11211 🚇 L: BEDFORD AVE ☎ 718.782.0332 ⊕ OSLOCOFFEE.COM

PARLOR COFFEE

Hidden in the back of mostly men's barbershop Persons of Interest's Williamsburg branch, this takeout counter doesn't offer skim milk, soy milk, or decaf, but it does serve delicious, deeply flavored coffee brewed from beans roasted in Brooklyn.

84 HAVEMEYER STREET . 11211 🚇 L: BEDFORD AVE ☎ 718.218.9100 ⊕ PARLORCOFFEE.COM

SWEETLEAF

This laid-back, spacious coffeehouse offers some extra-potent iced specialties, like Rocket Fuel, an appropriately named blend of java and maple syrup, as well as the customary selection of espresso drinks, tea, and baked items.

135 KENT AVENUE . 11211 🚇 L: BEDFORD AVE ☎ 347.725.4862 ⊕ SWEETLEAFLLC.COM

TOBY'S ESTATE COFFEE

On weekends there's a massive line outside this conveniently located spot, but it's busy almost all the time, due to its coffee (the beans of which are roasted on the premises), tasty light food (like the BLT, made with espresso-glazed bacon), and classes in various nuances of home brewing.

125 NORTH 6TH STREET . 11249 🚇 L: BEDFORD AVE ☎ 347.457.6170 ⊕ TOBYSESTATE.COM

Sweet William

There's a mystical quality to this kids' store that is as appealing to gift-buying young uncles and godparents as it is to children themselves. Conceived by Bronagh Staley, a former editor at the defunct upscale children's style magazine *Cookie*, the standout here is a virtual menagerie of stuffed animals from Germany's Hansa, one of Europe's best toymakers, scattered around the store, including in a huge treehouse-like wooden structure at the back. But there is also plenty of clothing—most of it organic and created by independent designers—that is hard to find elsewhere, like Bobo Choses—whose hipster-in-training tees make some adults wish they could squeeze into kidswear—and Popupshop. Sweet William's best for kids six and under, which also explains the stroller jam here at times, particularly on weekends.

324 WYTHE AVENUE . 11249 J/M/Z: MARCY AVE; L: BEDFORD AVE ☎ 718.218.6946
🌐 SWEETWILLIAMLTD.COM

Strawser + Smith

The antiques here come from many styles and eras, from ornate lamps from the 1940s to modernist tables to neoclassical sculptures by Italian-American artist Gaetano Cecere, but what makes this large home furnishings source stand out is its quirky pop-culture additions to that mix: a 1950s Harley-Davidson motorcycle, vintage manual typewriters in pristine condition, old signs and globes, and early 1960s storage racks. Located on a busy stretch of Driggs Avenue, the shop is a frequent stop for nonlocals strolling by on weekends as well as interior designers and other Brooklynites.

487 DRIGGS AVENUE . 11211 🚇 L: BEDFORD AVE ☎ 718.388.7600
🌐 STRAWSERANDSMITH.COM

Concrete + Water

Concrete + Water's sensibility is about ease and comfort, albeit with just-edgy-enough style that's in accordance with its location a few blocks from the Bedford Avenue subway station. That translates into dresses by brands like Sea and Whit in simple silhouettes but quirky fabrics, slouchy guys' separates from Shades of Grey by Micah Cohen and Rogue Territory, finishing-touch jewelry by Lizzie Fortunato, and small giftables from niche brands like Good Candle. There's a large outdoor space in back, in which the store hosts regular events, parties, and pop-up shops when the weather is warm.

485 DRIGGS AVENUE . 11211 🚇 L: BEDFORD AVE ☎ 917.909.1828
🌐 CONCRETEANDWATER.COM

242 Grand Street

This dark and vibey jewelry shop is a collective of three unconventional jewelers—Britt Bolton, Perry Gargano, and Dana Marie Burmeister—who sell their creations up front and share a large workshop in the back. The common denominator is an artistic touch that makes each piece quite distinctive, although the three disparate styles somehow harmoniously share the boutique space. Admittedly, the store has a touch of the foreboding atmosphere of a Nine Inch Nails music video—slightly goth, filled with pieces that would be best paired with black clothing and maybe some body piercing—but the friendliness of the designers, at least one of whom is usually here, makes up for it.

242 GRAND STREET . 11211   J/M/Z: MARCY AVE; L: BEDFORD AVE   ☎ 917.749.0566
🌐 BRITTBOLTON.COM . PERRYGARGANO.COM . DANAMARIEBURMEISTER.COM

Cotton Candy Machine

Think of this South Williamsburg store as an art gallery for shoppers that never thought they'd buy art, or even, perhaps, set foot into a space exhibiting it. On the walls hang vivid, accessibly priced artists' prints, often with a science-fiction/comic book spirit that appeals to the neighborhood's teen-at-heart twentysomething guys and specifically curated to look great on apartment walls nearby. Even more affordable is an array of other items for sale, like striking illustrated books, small collectible figurines, and wearables like t-shirts and baseball caps emblazoned with, yes, finely drawn artwork.

235 SOUTH 1ST STREET . 11211 🚇 G: METROPOLITAN AVE; J/M/Z: MARCY AVE; L: LORIMER ST
☎ 718.387.3844 ⊕ THECOTTONCANDYMACHINE.COM

Primp & Polish

With neat rows of more than one thousand nail polish colors lined up against the wall, Primp & Polish's handful of branches have become, for many women, the neighborhood's manicure and pedicure specialists of choice. There are five locations across Williamsburg and Greenpoint; this one is busy, bright, and—like the rest—spotless. The sensibility is a tad more upscale than at a typical no-frills New York City manicure spot; smile-inducing details include the option of Chanel and Dior polishes and a kid-size bubble gum pink treatment chair for young girls accompanying their moms. Although walk-ins are welcome, reservations are highly recommended on weekends and most weeknights.

205 NORTH 9TH STREET . 11211 🚇 L: BEDFORD AVE ☎ 718.965.1900
🌐 PRIMPANDPOLISH.COM

Pilgrim Surf + Supply

Surfboards might not be the first thing that comes to mind when you think of trendy Williamsburg, but there actually are a few noteworthy spots to hang ten relatively nearby, like Rockaway Beach in Queens. The impressive selection—in terms of size, details, and color—of boards at Pilgrim Surf + Supply belies the store's immediate urban surroundings and its clear view of the skyscraper-lined Manhattan skyline around the corner. Although there's serious surfers' gear for sale, landlubbers will find a concordant selection of guys' tees, hats, swim trunks, sneakers, and bags. To help set the mood, there's vintage bric-a-brac speckled throughout, plus a working turntable playing both new and old vinyl.

68 NORTH 3RD STREET . 11249 🚇 L: BEDFORD AVE ☎ 718.218.7456
🌐 PILGRIMSURFSUPPLY.COM

Greenpoint

To many New Yorkers, Greenpoint is "Little Poland," a predominantly immigrant-filled community, complete with bakeries specializing in poppy seed bread and restaurants serving large, inexpensive plates of hearty kielbasa. Poles began flocking to the area over a century ago, when it was a hub of factories manufacturing everything from drinking glasses to massive ships. There are still plenty of Polish residents and businesses—Rzeszowska Bakery, for example, is highly recommended, particularly for its worth-the-indulgence babka—but over the last few years there's been an influx of young creative types coming to live and work in the neighborhood. Here Poles and hipsters happily cohabitate; Greenpoint is less gentrified and crowded than Williamsburg and has a bit more of a small village feel. It's also attracted small business owners who have a particularly original vision, making it an ideal area to explore.

In God We Trust

In God We Trust's line of clothing for men and women is understated, utilitarian, not overly body-conscious, usually neutral in color, and chic without looking like it took any effort to get that way; in a sense, it's a New York City equivalent of the cult Parisian brand A.P.C. On the sassier side is its jewelry collection, made in a large workroom behind the cash desk, which includes heart-shaped pendants engraved with phrases like "bad bitch" and "sweet tits" and signet rings detailed with the outline of a Playboy bunny. For more meek wearers, the pieces are customizable with initials or words of one's choice. The jewelry is such a strongpoint that the store also offers commitment and engagement rings that can be personalized.

70 GREENPOINT AVENUE . 11222 🚇 G: GREENPOINT AVE ☎ 718.389.3546
🌐 INGODWETRUSTNYC.COM

Budin

Despite its location in a predominantly Polish neighborhood, this café and store's focus is Nordic, from the connoisseur coffee it serves from roasters like Norway's Tim Wendelboe to the home-skewed items for sale in the back, like vases from Finnish architect and designer Alvar Aalto. Some might say Budin reeks of gentrification, as it is more chic than other coffeehouses nearby, but it's hard not to love undeniably delicious snacks like Danish rye bread with smoked salmon and butter, and a staff that's friendly and relaxed—except about coffee preparation, which is all about intense precision.

114 GREENPOINT AVENUE . 11222 🚇 G: GREENPOINT AVE ☎ 347.844.9639
🌐 BUDIN-NYC.COM

Ovenly

Although this sparse little café is unquestionably cozy, the draw here isn't the atmosphere, but the irresistible and inventive baked goods. Particularly delicious are the scones, including a marvelously sharp version with cheddar cheese and mustard, and shortbread that's spiked with espresso and shards of caramelized sugar. Also tempting are deeply flavored dark chocolate brownies. Yet for all the buttery goodness of those treats, Ovenly also offers some quasi-healthy options—sure to delight even those who tend to shy away from sweets—that substitute indulgent ingredients with healthier alternatives, like splendidly chewy gluten-free pistachio cookies sweetened with agave and not-too-sweet vegan chocolate chip cookies. Although Ovenly's creations are sold at a wide range of leading cafés in the area and the weekly Smorgasburg market, the selection is most comprehensive here at its flagship shop.

31 GREENPOINT AVENUE . 11222 🚇 G: GREENPOINT AVE ☎ 347.689.3608
🌐 OVEN.LY

Line & Label

With Siouxsie and the Banshees blaring in the background and clothes by the likes of Christian Joy—a stylist who's worked with the Yeah Yeah Yeahs and Alabama Shakes—it's no surprise that the garments at this homespun boutique have a rock 'n' roll edge. But owner Kate O'Riley, who designs some of the clothing, offers pieces that would work in a casual office environment despite their "cool girl" sensibility. There's also restrained, delicate jewelry and simple bags to tone things down. Nothing's too pricey and many items, including just-trendy-enough handbags, are made in-house in a studio that's tucked in back.

568 MANHATTAN AVENUE . 11222 🚇 G: NASSAU AVE; L: BEDFORD AVE ☎ 347.384.2678
🌐 LINEANDLABEL.COM

Bellocq Tea Atelier

Standing inside this truly inviting space, surrounded by bright yellow tea canisters and fragrant samples of tea leaves, you'd never guess what's beyond the front door: an industrial block near the water that's desolate, windy, and anything but quaint. But the interior's feel, more Rive Gauche than Rive Greenpoint, perfectly fits its offerings: unusual blends of top-quality tea, packaged beautifully. There's a large selection: standouts include Kikuya, organic green sencha mixed with Bulgarian rose essence, and Le Hammeau, an herbal mix with lavender and mint. If you need help deciding what to buy, extra-knowledgeable staff are happy to patiently advise.

104 WEST STREET . 11222 🚇 G: GREENPOINT AVE ☎ 347.463.9231
🌐 BELLOCQ.COM

WORD

It's not all that big, but this book lovers' bookshop offers an impressively comprehensive range of volumes that skews toward the neighborhood and the interests of its tastemakers. There are paperback novels by young writers and classic writers, books about critically acclaimed rock bands, some local travel guides, clever greeting cards, and a small nook of kids' books in the back. It's also a focal point in the community, engaging people through book groups, comedy nights, a basketball team, and even a matchmaking bulletin board that harks back to the days when personal ads appeared in print. In addition, the shop is open until 9 P.M. every night, making it easy to pick up essential reads on the way home from work or after an evening cocktail at Black Rabbit, a popular pub that's a few blocks away.

126 FRANKLIN AVENUE . 11222   G: GREENPOINT AVE   ☎ 718.383.0096

🌐 WORDBOOKSTORES.COM

WORDS
FOR
NERDS
a book of the month club
... sci-fi / fantasy readers

Acme Smoked Fish

Since 1906, this family-owned and -run operation has been supplying smoked fish to New York City businesses that have built their reputations on its quality, like Barney Greengrass and Zabar's. On Friday mornings, Acme opens up its no-frills headquarters to the public, laying out copious amounts of smoked salmon and other delicacies at wholesale prices. Plan on arriving early: doors open at 8 A.M., and there's usually a steadily flowing line all morning, in which neighborhood hipsters, foodies, and longtime Polish residents all stand together, waiting to get into the shop. It's especially crowded before major holidays, when people stock up for festive meals. Acme accepts cash only.

30 GEM STREET . 11222 🚇 G: NASSAU AVE ☎ 718.383.8585
🌐 ACMESMOKEDFISH.COM

Five Leaves

The publike Australian feel of this welcoming spot isn't a mere coincidence: it was cofounded by the late actor Heath Ledger, who lived in Brooklyn for several years before he passed away. He's to thank for its name as well, a nod to the title of an album by cult singer-songwriter Nick Drake. Five Leaves is packed literally all day, mostly with a neighborhood crowd that comes for updated comfort dishes like herb-crusted duck and smoked trout rarebit. When it's sunny, a handful of outdoor café tables offer al fresco dining, although the view from the bottom of Bedford Avenue is admittedly more about people watching than picturesque scenery.

18 BEDFORD AVENUE . 11222   🚇 G: NASSAU AVE   ☎ 718.383.5345

🌐 FIVELEAVESNY.COM

Wolves Within

Wolves Within opened as Greenpoint's retail scene was just emerging, and most garments sold in the area were either trendy or vintage. The selection here is neither: everything has a lived-in casualness that's unpretentious. For guys, there are Save Khaki pants, easy button-downs by Alex Mill, and Vans; for women, there are slender jeans by Objects Without Meaning and striated-pattern scarves woven on antique looms. Nearly everything here is made in America, a priority for the owners when choosing what to carry.

174 FRANKLIN STREET . 11222 🚇 G: GREENPOINT AVE ☎ 347.889.5798
🌐 WOLVESWITHIN.COM

Home of the Brave

The sister store of Wolves Within, this bright, sparse space applies its worn yet unaffected aesthetic to items for the home that readily work as gifts. Like its counterpart, Home of the Brave carries mostly items made in America, with other pieces thrown into the mix, like rugs crafted by Guatemalan artisans that are so beautiful they seem destined to be displayed as artwork—as they are in the shop—rather than on the floor. The wide selection of appealing items—handmade mugs, smooth pastel-colored vases, pretty greeting cards—makes the shop particularly popular with Manhattanites who've ventured into the neighborhood as well as locals who bring out-of-town friends and relatives.

146 FRANKLIN STREET . 11222 🚇 G: GREENPOINT AVE ☎ 347.384.2776
🌐 HOMEOFTHEBRAVENYC.COM

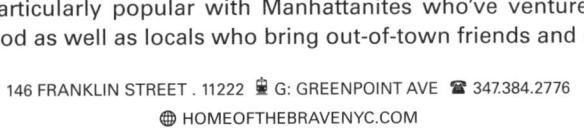

94.95

Cotter Barber

Over the last few years, there's been an influx of hipster barbershops—complete with old-school chairs for customers and, in many cases, a counter for lattes as you wait for a trim—in Brooklyn's trendier neighborhoods. Greenpoint is no exception. Cotter Barber is a convivial spot that offers the chairs and connoisseur's coffee but not one iota of attitude, welcoming customers into a comfortable space detailed with reclaimed wood that feels relaxed, not posey. There's a serene outdoor space with plantings and minimal furnishings at the back—where you can wait for a straight-razor shave or snack on an Ovenly pastry afterward—and a cross-section of hard-to-find beauty lines for sale, like Sweden's L:A Bruket and California's Earth Tu Face alongside better-known brands like Proraso and Taylor of Old Bond Street.

563 MANHATTAN AVENUE . 11222   G: NASSAU AVE; L: BEDFORD AVE   ☎ 347.987.4562

🌐 COTTER.NYC

Suite Pieces

Tucked on a side street near one of Greenpoint's main subway stations, Suite Pieces is a hybrid: part crafty paint store, part vintage bric-a-brac boutique. People in the neighborhood stop in to pick up cute and sometimes kitschy small tabletop items—candlesticks, vases, bookends—culled mostly from estate sales on Long Island, where the store has two much larger locations. (This one's a 425-square-foot sliver, smaller even than some Big Apple apartments.) The attraction for shoppers from all over New York City is Annie Sloan Chalk Paint, a special variety that's extra-easy to use and doesn't require sanding or professional know-how, so even novices can spiff up inexpensive flea market furniture finds. Also popular are the shop's workshop classes and one-on-one instruction sessions that teach customers various decorative techniques and design tricks.

162 HURON STREET . 11222 🚇 G: GREENPOINT AVE ☎ 347.987.3586
🌐 SUITEPIECES.COM

Glasserie

The name of this unpretentious, warm restaurant isn't just a coincidence: the building was built in 1860 and originally housed a large factory that made lighting fixtures and other glassware. The décor nods to that heritage—with framed drawings of period buildings and antique lights, some of which depict pieces actually made in the space—but the cuisine is 100 percent modern, revolving around seasonal, locally sourced produce that's mostly light, healthy, and somewhat inspired by the Middle East, where owner Sara Conklin grew up. In spite of being a bit removed from busier Manhattan Avenue, the restaurant attracts diners from all over New York City, especially for weekend brunch, which includes a massive (and massively delicious) mezze platter that's designed for sharing.

95 COMMERCIAL STREET . 11222 🚇 G: GREENPOINT AVE ☎ 718.389.0640
🌐 GLASSERIENYC.COM

THIS
CANDLE
SMELLS
LIKE
MAGNOLIA

THIS
CANDLE
SMELLS
LIKE
NIGHTSHADE

THIS
CANDLE
SMELLS
LIKE
FLINT

Oak

The aesthetic of this industrial-feeling store, which also has locations in Manhattan, Los Angeles, and Paris, revolves around urban warrior wear that is tough, confident, and mostly devoid of color—unless, that is, you count black, the predominant hue of the majority of what's on the racks. Along those lines, there are updated biker jackets for men and women, slouchy tees, extra-lean and dark jeans, and hardy boots designed for walking city streets. Admittedly, some of its pieces are quite impactful when worn together for a head-to-toe look, but Oak is an ideal place to pick up a key item or two with a healthy dose of street-smart attitude.

55 NASSAU AVENUE . 11222 🚇 G: NASSAU AVE ☎ 718.782.0521
🌐 OAKNYC.COM

Luddite Antiques

It's easy to find reproductions of period lighting fixtures in large home furnishing retailers; this insiders' secret shop on a quiet section of Franklin Avenue sells the real thing. Co-owners Luke Scarola and Rebecca Squiers stock everything from hundred-year-old desk lamps to giant light-up industrial signs in a cluttered store that's not glamorous, but nonetheless has become a regular haunt of interior decorators as well as film and television set designers looking for items to insure the scenes they're working on look authentic. A minority of pieces here is sold more for display than actual lighting, but if one is of interest, the store can usually help get it in working order for an additional charge.

201 FRANKLIN STREET . 11222 🚇 G: GREENPOINT AVE; 7: VERNON BLVD–JACKSON AVE
☎ 718.387.3450 ⊕ LUDDITEANTIQUES.COM

People of 2Morrow

There's a bit of a hippie-ish patina to this large store—with incense burning and Native American sage smudge sticks for sale in a big wooden bowl—but there's something for just about everyone here: vintagewear for men and women, hefty clay Saint Karen pitchers and mugs, delicate little gold rings, prettily bound notebooks, Malaya organic body oil and incense made from Amazonian resin, and even some clothing for babies and small kids. With the neighborhood's cool-kid residents in mind, prices are comparatively low and the atmosphere is conducive to leisurely browsing.

65 FRANKLIN STREET . 11222 🚇 G: GREENPOINT AVE ☎ 718.383.4402
🌐 PEOPLEOF2MORROW.COM

Bushwick

Not so long ago, most New Yorkers wouldn't have considered Bushwick an enviable place to go shopping or dining: it was a rough-and-tumble neighborhood that—particularly at night, after its industrial factories had closed—could feel desolate and dangerous. What began as an affluent neighborhood a century ago, became a predominantly working-class Italian community in the 1950s, then weathered trying times before its recent resurgence. A steadily growing influx of artists has turned the area around, infusing it with an almost tangible creative buzz as well as many new businesses. That flood of new residents has also drastically improved the area's look: nearly every spare wall and steel grate is covered with street art, often in the form of huge, colorful murals. On a sunny day you'll see plenty of smartphone-toting visitors snapping photos of the bright graffiti to post on Facebook or Instagram as well as a person or two carrying a designer bag. Nonetheless, the neighborhood feels decidedly less gentrified than Williamsburg, which sits to its north and is closer to Manhattan.

Tomahawk Salon

For this creatively fueled neighborhood's artists, musicians, and writers, Tomahawk is *the* place for hair color, particularly if you're into the latest trends, from ombré in the extreme to various shades of blue, purple, and pink. For more conventional types, the salon and its all-female, tattooed and pierced staff might seem a bit intimidating, but they are actually very approachable and warm. Less bold hair colors and haircuts are also offered for both men and women, as well as nail art by Fleury Rose, a well-known manicurist who's worked with singers like Iggy Azalea and St. Vincent. In addition to styling treatments, there's a hodgepodge of items on sale up front that are in sync with the salon's punky aesthetic, like tattoo-inspired tees from Sourpuss Clothing.

17 THAMES STREET . 11206 🚇 L: MORGAN AVE ☎ 646.399.6873
🌐 TOMAHAWKSALON.COM

Martin Greenfield Clothiers

Decades before Bushwick became a cutting-edge oasis for graffiti artists and chefs cooking with locally sourced produce, Martin Greenfield was sewing suits by hand for some of the most influential movers and shakers from New York City and beyond. Years later, power brokers still schlep to this unassuming atelier up a couple flights of stairs; frequently, their idling chauffeur-driven cars are the easiest way to spot this otherwise-anonymous building. The clientele has included a handful of United States presidents and former New York City mayor Michael Bloomberg; mere civilians rely on his creations for the perfect suit for milestone events like weddings or, if employed in a formal office, everyday wear. The suits are milestone-priced, too, averaging a few thousand dollars each. You won't find fashion-forward designs here, but, for men's suiting, it's one of the best places in the country.

239 VARET STREET . 11206 🚇 L: MORGAN AVE ☎ 718.497.5480
🌐 GREENFIELDCLOTHIERS.COM

Fitzcarraldo

Rustic Italian food is not the first thing that comes to mind walking on Bushwick's many industrial-building-lined streets, but that's what Fitzcarraldo offers in a setting that's surprisingly conducive to quiet dinners, particularly on date night. The must-have dish here is farinella—an earthy chickpea flour pancake, daubed with either rosemary or pesto and roasted tomatoes and served in a cast-iron skillet—that's an ideal appetizer or bar snack with a glass of Nebbiolo or Birra Moretti. But everything here is prepared with extra-fresh ingredients and integrity, as it is at the owner's sister restaurant in Boerum Hill, Rucola.

195 MORGAN AVENUE . 11227 🚇 L: MORGAN AVE ☎ 718.233.2566
🌐 FITZBK.COM

Roberta's

This always-crowded restaurant is, ultimately, the culinary epicenter of Bushwick, pulling in people from, well, just about everywhere. The main attraction is pizza—doughy, wood-oven-baked, and served with salient toppings like littleneck clams, lemon, and Calabrian chilies. Like all the pies here, that one, which also has mozzarella, has a clever name: the Mermaid Parade, named after the annual costume-fueled festival in Coney Island. But there's much more than pizza on offer—like a winter lunchtime salad of warm sweet potatoes flecked with pumpkin seeds and vadouvan—and it's pretty much all original, mostly locally sourced, and delicious. There's nearly always a wait for a table—even when there's additional seating in back when weather permits—but this is one of those rare places that is really, truly worth the delay. On the other hand, insiders try to come early, opt for weekday lunch, or simply get their pies and sides to go instead.

261 MOORE STREET . 11206 🚇 L: MORGAN AVE ☎ 718.417.1118

🌐 ROBERTASPIZZA.COM

Friends NYC

Originally called Mary Meyer Clothing, this spacious store is now, as the name implies, a partnership between Mary Meyer and Emma Kadar-Penner. Meyer showcases her designs here, which are perfect for wannabe rock stars and the cool girls who aspire to dress like them. Black is, unsurprisingly, a prevalent color here, but the leggings, little dresses, and tank tops also come in attention-grabbing patterns that stand out, even if your stage is simply the Bushwick sidewalk outside. There are also a smattering of items from other brands, like pouches by BAGGU and darkly tinted sunglasses by M. Costa. The rest of the space is dedicated to vintagewear selected by Penner that complements Meyer's confident creations.

56 BOGART STREET . 11206 🚇 L: MORGAN AVE ☎ 718.386.6279

🌐 SHOPFRIENDSNYC.COM

The Narrows

Named after the strip of water that separates Brooklyn from Staten Island, this popular spot looks like what might be a film noir detective's favorite bar, circa 1935. Despite the dark atmospheric interior, the best seats here are outdoors, in a large backyard filled with flea market chairs and, on just about any warm evening, a huge throng of people. There's beer on tap and wine, but the drinks of choice are the cocktails, ranging from the basic (piquant daiquiris; an Americano made with vermouth, Campari, and soda) to the more complex (the surprisingly smooth Derringer, which includes Bulleit Bourbon and kava). Two other draws: the way-better-than-typical bar food menu of snacks—especially popcorn with cardamom and toffee as well as an herbaceous goat cheese dip—and its hours, which stretch to 4 A.M.

1037 FLUSHING AVENUE . 11237 🚇 L: MORGAN AVE ☎ 718.303.2047
🌐 NARROWSBAR.COM

Boerum Hill, Carroll Gardens, and Cobble Hill

These adjacent neighborhoods have distinct personalities but share the unmistakable air of a tight-knit community, with residents sitting on brownstone stoops chatting, restaurants where regular customers are known by name, and inviting small boutiques run by owners who live nearby.

Boerum Hill's property has become prime real estate, but the area was once more multicultural, with a mix of Arabs, Indians, African-Americans, and some native Brooklynites. Its main commercial row, Smith Street, is now a buzzing spot for food and fashion. Carroll Gardens's Italian heritage lingers in the many scrumptious reminders that have been made daily there for decades, like the chocolate-chip-studded cannoli at F. Monteleone Bakery & Cafe; the lobster tails, or *sfogliatelle*, at Court Pastry Shop; and coffee at D'Amico Coffee Roasters. Cobble Hill is perhaps the most affluent of the trio, with large homes and charming carriage houses, and Cobble Hill Park, where local kids play and adults come to unwind.

Bien Cuit

Equal parts neighborhood café and working bakery—complete with the scent of baked goods wafting from the back—Bien Cuit's French feel goes beyond its name, which translates as "well done," referring to the darker-than-average crust of its breads. The croissants, baguettes, and almond sablés here taste authentically French and are offered as part of a longer list of carbtastic breads, quiches, and treats that changes with the season. But not every irresistible offering has a Parisian accent: other noteworthy delectables include a take on *tebirke*, a flaky Danish pastry filled with almond paste and topped with poppy seeds, and the Sicilian, a savory tomato-studded tartlet.

120 SMITH STREET . 11201 🚇 A/C/G: HOYT–SCHERMERHORN; F/G: BERGEN ST; 2/3: HOYT ST
☎ 718.852.0200 🌐 BIENCUIT.COM

Fork & Pencil

The jumble of antique items at this Court Street mainstay isn't organized or logical in arrangement, but that doesn't make the fairly priced array any less appealing. There are all sorts of jewelry—precious and semiprecious rings and necklaces and brooches—and china, including ornate plates and dainty cups and saucers. In back is a small room dedicated to kids' items; it's less serious and even more accessibly priced than the store's main array. As further enticement to shop, Fork & Pencil donates profits to a variety of worthy local charities. The store also operates a larger warehouse space a few blocks away, at 18 Bergen Street.

221 COURT STREET . 11201 🚇 F/G BERGEN ST; 2/3/4/5: BOROUGH HALL ☎ 718.488.8855
🌐 FORKANDPENCIL.COM

Article &

Once known as Dear Fieldbinder, Article & is an unassuming boutique that offers exactly what women in the neighborhood want: fuss-free clothes with just enough of a designery touch to feel fashionable but never forced or fleeting. The shop has a loyal clientele, who come back for pieces that pair as naturally with jeans on weekends as with something a bit more polished for the office, albeit most likely one with a relatively relaxed dress code. In addition to separates from easy-to-pull-off brands likes Cheap Monday and Lauren Moffatt, there's a bit of similarly restrained but on-point jewelry, well-priced footwear, just-sexy-enough underpinnings by Eberjey, and delicately scented candles by Joya and Tatine.

198 SMITH STREET . 11201 🚇 F/G: BERGEN ST ☎ 718.852.3620
🌐 ARTICLEAND.COM

Horseman Antiques

For vintage furniture junkies who could happily spend hours rummaging around flea markets looking for unusual finds, this massive store might well be described as paradise. On five somewhat cacophonous floors that stretch over 25,000 square feet, Horseman, which has been in business since 1962, piles a huge array of very beautiful antique furniture pieces, from mirrored art deco desks to wooden cigar store Indians to midcentury art and sculptures. The place is not all that well organized, so allow plenty of time for a visit. Pieces are, for the most part, in excellent shape, and the prices are not stratospheric.

351 ATLANTIC AVENUE . 11217 🚇 A/C/G: HOYT–SCHERMERHORN ☎ 718.596.1048
🌐 HORSEMANANTIQUES.NET

Brooklyn Social

Walking up Smith Street, it's easy to miss Brooklyn Social: instead of the large logo you might expect on the front of a neighborhood bar, there's simply a tiny sign reading "Non-members welcome." Once you walk in, the space really does feel quite clubby—and was, for many years, the meeting place of *Societa Risposto*, a Sicilian men's group—but this fabulously dark establishment is simply a bar that relishes the warm, cigarette-stained feel of a classic 1950s watering hole. To maintain that atmosphere, there's a bulky vintage cash register, yellowed antique photos, and a jukebox playing oldies by Patsy Cline, Irma Thomas, and Serge Gainsbourg. The drink of choice for many is the perfectly blended Negroni, best sipped while shooting pool in a small room at the back.

335 SMITH STREET . 11231 🚇 F/G: CARROLL ST ☎ 718.858.7758
🌐 BROOKLYNSOCIALBAR.COM

Flight 001

Whether you're heading for a long journey abroad or taking a day trip to the Hamptons, this store's got you covered, stocking both travel essentials like lightweight wheelie suitcases and less requisite gear like, well, a boxed set of chopsticks to tuck into your bag for sushi to go. The sweet spot: smaller items that can help make a cramped economy seat feel more like flying in first class: cushioned black-out eye masks, inflatable pillows, crisp and colorful passport holders, and little cases to keep everything you've packed clean and organized. Plenty here has a sense of fun—like luggage tags that read "My private jet is in the shop"—so it's also a reliable source of gifts.

132 SMITH STREET . 11201 🚇 F/G: BERGEN ST ☎ 718.243.0001
🌐 FLIGHT001.COM

Café Pedlar

There's nothing slick about the atmosphere of this compact café, which, with its basic seating and neighborhood regulars, feels like it's been a Cobble Hill staple for generations although it opened in 2009. That unpretentiousness is part of its appeal, as is hot chocolate made from homemade ganache, Stumptown Hair Bender blend coffee, and buttery croissants and cookies. The caliber of the food and drinks comes as no surprise: Pedlar shares owners with Brooklyn foodie-favorite Frankie's 457, whose sharp Sicilian olive oil is sold here, among a few other pantry items, and German-inspired farm-to-table specialists Prime Meats. Unlike a lot of cafés, you won't find too many laptop-bound, headphone-wearing workers here, but rather families, friends getting together, and coffee drinkers reading a hardcover book or newspaper at leisure.

210 COURT STREET . 11201 🚇 F/G: BERGEN ST; 2/3/4/5: BOROUGH HALL ☎ 718.855.7129
🌐 CAFEPEDLAR.COM

Coffee Shop
Cafe Pedlar
Coffee
Espresso
Hot Tea
Hot Chocolate

Hunting with Jake

The mix of mostly home-related items at this store is quite broad, yet somehow always coherent, juxtaposing vintage desktop globes, brass bookends, and sets of chairs with new birdcage-like hanging lamps, Woolrich totes, jewelry in silver and gold embedded with semiprecious stones, and compelling outsider art by Alabama-based Butch Anthony. The shop feels more like a labor-of-love boutique in a stylish weekend community than an urban retailer, although just about everything here would work well in a nearby apartment. There are also more housewarming-sized gifts than at some other Atlantic Avenue furnishing stores; it's a reliable spot for ornate ashtrays, Clark & Henry soaps, Roland Pine scented candles and diffusers, and coffee table books.

380 ATLANTIC AVENUE . 11217 🚇 A/C/G: HOYT–SCHERMERHORN; 2/3/4/5: NEVINS ST ☎ 718.522.6075
🌐 HUNTINGWITHJAKE.COM

Barneys New York

Like its sister locations in Manhattan and beyond, the Brooklyn branch of Barneys New York stocks an urbane and covetable mix of high-end designerwear for men and women. The duplex space is expansive but not overwhelmingly large, with women's items upstairs and men's below. In sync with the store's size, the edit's a bit tighter and a touch more casual here than at the Manhattan flagship, but still includes loads of major names (Alexander Wang, Phillip Lim, Isabel Marant, Comme des Garçons, and many others), bags, jewelry, a small shoe selection, and even beautifiers from La Mer and makeup artist Troy Surratt. Prices are steep, but deals can still be found during the store's biannual sales, usually in late June and late December.

194 ATLANTIC AVENUE . 11201 🚇 2/3/4/5: BOROUGH HALL ☎ 718.637.2234
🌐 BARNEYS.COM

Moscot

This compact Brooklyn location of Moscot—a century-old, family-run New York City optician with several other branches—is a relatively new addition to the neighborhood, but the shop feels as if it's been there for generations. Some of that is due to the attention to subtle detail regarding its displays—eyeglass trays that are ceramic instead of plastic, mannequins papier-mâchéd with vintage newspaper ads—but, really, it's due to loyal customers. Those in the neighborhood know they can rely on the store for precisely filled prescriptions in high-quality frames. In addition, many of the frames have an antiquated look that's cool without seeming forced or hokey, hence the brand's appeal to high-profile types, including Johnny Depp.

159 COURT STREET . 11201 🚇 F/G: BERGEN ST; 2/3/4/5: BOROUGH HALL ☎ 718.551.0591
🌐 MOSCOT.COM

By Brooklyn

This comprehensive Carroll Gardens boutique carries only items that are made in the borough: Raaka Chocolate's artisanal bars, Brooklyn Delhi's fabulously hot tomato achaar, Apotheke soaps, Papersheep letterpress cards, and even headphones by Sunset Park–based Grado Labs. There are also plenty of souvenir-ready items, all with a refreshing twist, like pencils printed with lines from songs extolling the area's virtues like the Beastie Boys' "No Sleep Till Brooklyn," and Maptote's cotton bags silk-screened with maps of the borough. With this attractive mix of goods, the store has become a mainstay with locals and a real draw for tourists. Owner Gaia DiLoreto has also become the community's de facto earth mother for young entrepreneurs, offering advice on manufacturing and consulting with the area's Chamber of Commerce to certify key local businesses as "Brooklyn Made." By Brooklyn has a second location in Williamsburg at 142 Grand Street.

261 SMITH STREET . 11231 🚇 F/G: BERGEN ST; 2/3/4/5: BOROUGH HALL ☎ 718.643.0606

🌐 BYBROOKLYN.COM

Black Gold Records

Although it's not in the busiest part of Carroll Gardens, this coffee bar, antique store, and vintage record dealer is in a truly prime location: sandwiched between Frankies 457 and Prime Meats, two acclaimed local restaurants. For many, the draw is the vinyl, spanning a variety of genres and eras and restocked very regularly. A couple times a year there's a special $1 sale on albums, for which the line extends out of the door and around the block. The vintage items for sale are mostly kitschy and a touch macabre—medical models and taxidermy, among them. The coffee is strong and tasty—made with beans from New Jersey's Rook Coffee Roasters—and there are also baked goods from local purveyors like Ovenly.

461 COURT STREET . 11231 🚇 F/G: SMITH–9TH STS ☎ 347.227.8227
🌐 BLACKGOLDBROOKLYN.COM

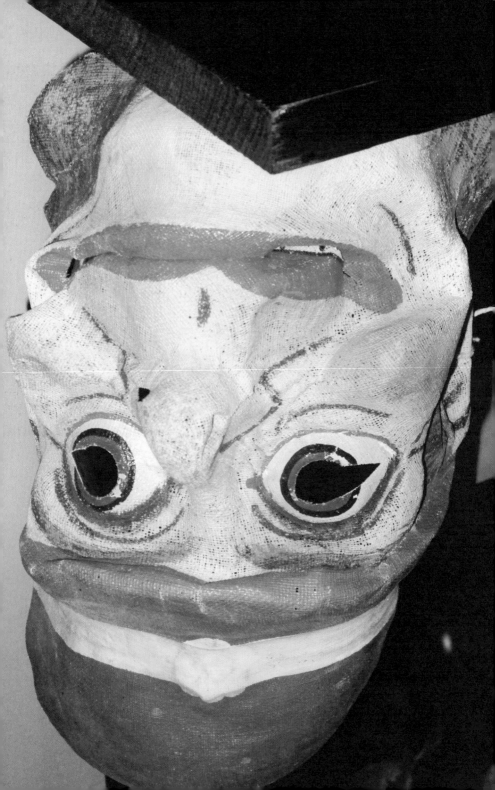

SHEN Beauty

There's no need for Cobble Hill residents to go to a Manhattan department store to find unique beauty products thanks to SHEN Beauty, which brings together brands that mostly have been discovered by the shop owner, and are often locally made, eco-friendly, or an exclusive import for which you'd need to take a trip abroad and have an in-the-know friend to find. That includes makeup from By Terry, skincare by British facialist Amanda Lacey, lipsticks by Troi Ollivierre, Phylia shampoo and conditioner, REN cleansers, Ellis Brooklyn body milks, and Jin Soon nail polish, all presented in a way that's approachable and unintimidating. Services like facials are offered, too, which help encourage loyal regulars to linger as well as come again.

315 COURT STREET . 11231 🚇 F/G: CARROLL ST; 2/3/4/5: BOROUGH HALL ☎ 718.576.2679
🌐 SHEN-BEAUTY.COM

Steven Alan

This visionary Manhattan-based retailer's Atlantic Avenue boutiques offer clothing and accessories—relaxed, a tad insouciant, cosmopolitan but not too polished or assertive—that resonate deeply with stylish Brooklynites. The two stores (one for men, one for women) stock upscale urban essentials like soft cotton button-downs, hefty winter parkas, and semi-structured blazers from Alan's own cohesive line as well as clothing by designers that share the brand's sensibility, like Acne, Carven, and A.P.C. The assortment includes many options but is never overwhelming, making the store a place that even people who hate to shop for clothes look forward to stopping by. There's also a newer store that's focused on home items nearby at 373 Atlantic Avenue.

347 AND 349 ATLANTIC AVENUE . 11217 🚇 A/C/G: HOYT–SCHERMERHORN; F/G: BERGEN ST
☎ 347.382.9125; 718.852.3257 ⊕ STEVENALAN.COM

BookCourt

This well-stocked bookstore encourages readers to browse, ask for suggestions, and linger, which usually doesn't take much arm-twisting, especially since a great portion of the store lies within a large, sun-infused room with a skylit ceiling, the remains of a greenhouse the owners renovated when they expanded the space into what was once a flower shop next door. BookCourt hosts a full schedule of personal appearances by all sorts of authors every week—in fact, almost every night—along with book clubs. As has been the case since it opened more than three decades ago, BookCourt has a highly comprehensive selection of fiction for a neighborhood bookshop, including new novels, classics, and more obscure but equally worthy reads. It's also very strong in nonfiction and cookbooks, and always carries a smattering of interesting art, photography, design, and Brooklyn-centric volumes.

163 COURT STREET . 11201 🚇 F/G: BERGEN ST; 2/3/4/5: BOROUGH HALL ☎ 718.875.3677
🌐 BOOKCOURT.COM

PasParTou

There's an unassuming feel to this impulse-purchase-friendly boutique, a few doors down from the popular Cafe Pedlar on a bustling section of Court Street. The array of items is both unpretentious and diverse, from pretty hand-painted cobalt blue serving platters to funky woven friendship bracelets detailed with the word "Brooklyn." There are quite a few pithy borough-centric items, like mugs with Cobble Hill's zip code, which make ideal souvenirs, even if they simply end up on a mantelpiece a few blocks away. But there are elegant items on offer, too, like glassware imported from Poland that you won't see elsewhere in the United States. Somehow, it all makes sense together, and nothing is too extreme or expensive. That hard-to-pull-off coherence comes down to the eye of store owner Gosia Rojek, who has lived in a nearby brownstone for almost three decades and has an inherent understanding of what speaks to the community.

206 COURT STREET . 11201 🚇 F/G: BERGEN ST; 2/3/4/5: BOROUGH HALL ☎ 718.422.7700
🌐 PAS-PAR-TOU.COM

La Vara

On a quiet and residential block of brownstones sits La Vara, a small restaurant you might logically assume to be a modest neighborhood spot for an easy weeknight dinner out. But the food here is exceptional, and worth traveling from way beyond Cobble Hill for. The cuisine is Moorish—Spanish with some Jewish and Moroccan influences—so the dishes are served tapas-style, designed to be shared and ordered in bulk. Not to miss are carabineros— giant lipstick-red shrimp from Spain that are nearly langoustines, grilled with preserved lemon—and the regular special of squid-dotted thick almond gazpacho. Although dinner's the main attraction here, there's also an inventive brunch, at which eggs are paired with squid, chorizo, and garlicky lamb hash.

268 CLINTON STREET . 11201   🚇 F/G: BERGEN ST; 2/3/4/5: BOROUGH HALL   ☎ 718.422.0065
🌐 LAVARANY.COM

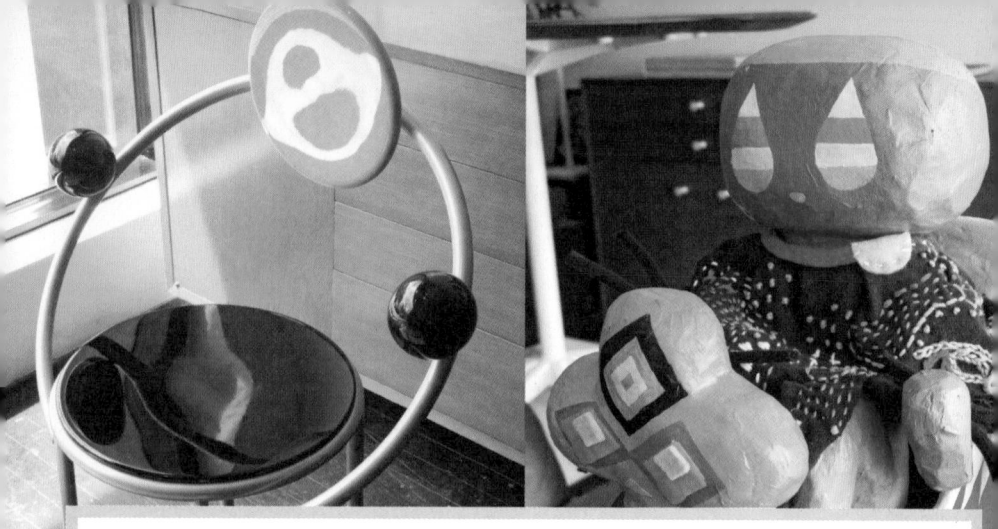

Bright Lyons

This spunky high-end vintage home store stocks the big names you'd expect from a midcentury specialist—George Nelson, Herman Miller, Ettore Sottsass—and some you might not, like 1960s textile designer Alexander Girard, whose hard-to-find, über-collectible, massive stretches of multi-hued printed fabric are often available here. As the store's name implies, color is a leitmotif at Bright Lyons, which makes it feel somewhat less serious than some of Atlantic Avenue's other furniture stores, although the selection here is investment-tiered, with prices to match.

383 ATLANTIC AVENUE . 11217 🚇 A/C/G: HOYT–SCHERMERHORN ☎ 718.855.5463
🌐 BRIGHTLYONS.COM

Persons of Interest

You might logically assume that Persons of Interest, the mostly men's barbershop, was open when bell-bottoms were in vogue; after all, there's a big 1970s-style mural against one wall and three antique barber chairs that make it seem as if the shop was in business long before that. It is actually in a space that was previously a no-frills neighborhood barber—the mural is a relic from that era—but the cuts here are definitely up-to-date. It's especially popular with guys in their twenties and thirties who live nearby, but the shop's unintimidating vibe of cool appeals to a broad range of clients, including more than a few women. There are also locations at 82–84 Havemeyer Street in Williamsburg and at 88 South Portland Street in Fort Greene.

299 SMITH STREET . 11231   F/G: CARROLL ST   ☎ 718.858.5300
🌐 PERSONSOFINTERESTBKLYN.COM

Twisted Lily

Choosing a perfume you really love can be a challenge; finding one that's so unique you won't smell it on anyone else can seem like an impossible dream. That's where Twisted Lily comes in, stocking fragrance lines you probably haven't heard of—in a bright space that's neither intimidating nor overly swank—and encouraging customers to test the many scents. You won't find Chanel No. 5 here, but here you will find all sorts of niche perfume brands, some comparatively well known—like Comme des Garçons, Arquiste, Serge Lutens, and Penhaligon's—and some less familiar for most shoppers—like Grossmith, Olfactive Studio, and Histoires de Parfums. The offerings span a broad price range, so there are more accessible treats than you might expect in a room filled with so many imported and artisanal scents.

360 ATLANTIC AVENUE . 11217 🚇 A/C/G: HOYT–SCHERMERHORN ☎ 347.529.4681
🌐 TWISTEDLILY.COM

Erica Weiner

One of this born-in-Brooklyn jeweler's specialties is engagement rings and wedding bands that aren't overly formal or pricey, whether they're vintage or one of Weiner's own vintage-inspired designs. There's also plenty for those who are single: on-trend stud earrings, pendants made from old New York City subway tokens, and affordable solitaire rings focused around a single jagged and striated quartz crystal are part of the draw for browsers and beyond, particularly those who stroll down Atlantic Avenue on busy weekends.

360 ATLANTIC AVENUE . 11217 🚇 A/C/G: HOYT–SCHERMERHORN ☎ 718.855.2555
🌐 ERICAWEINER.COM

Eva Gentry Consignment

At any given time, Eva Dayton's well-stocked Atlantic Avenue store carries women's designers like Chanel, Céline, Dries Van Noten, Christian Louboutin, and many others, all sold at a fraction of what you'd pay in a Madison Avenue boutique. Everything is previously owned—sometimes new-with-tags, sometimes a bit worn but in excellent condition—and sourced mostly from the closets of women who live nearby. Like many shops of this ilk, pieces are organized by color and offered seasonally, so it's easy to come in on a hunt for, say, a lightweight black dress, and see the choice in a quick glance. The store is also active on social media sites like Instagram, where some shoppers research new arrivals before they stop by.

371 ATLANTIC AVENUE . 11217 🚇 A/C/G: HOYT–SCHERMERHORN ☎ 718.522.3522

🌐 EVAGENTRYCONSIGNMENT.COM

Brooklyn Heights

Walking down Brooklyn Heights' quiet residential streets lined with enormous nineteenth-century brownstones that haven't changed very much over the years, it's easy to imagine that you've stepped back in time or onto a film set, as the neighborhood's atmospheric streets and stately promenade have appeared in *Annie Hall*, *The Age of Innocence*, and *Moonstruck*, among others. The area isn't locked in a time warp, though; it's one of the borough's most centrally located neighborhoods, an easy walk to the downtown area, with its many retail businesses, municipal offices, and subway lines. There's also a main commercial drag, Montague Street, where a few much-loved independent boutiques and restaurants have long thrived beside branches of Kiehl's, M.A.C, and Banana Republic. On the more residential streets, small businesses—a café here, an artisan's shop there—are peppered among the homes. On weekday afternoons, expect to see candy-eating kids walking from Saint Ann's School, a well-known private academy that's been in the neighborhood since 1965.

Tango

Brooklyn Heights is not one of the borough's trendier parts; with its community's sense of style in mind, this attitude-free store has been offering comfortable, polished women's clothing and accessories since 1970. The selection of uncomplicated pieces includes not-overly-detailed dresses by Diane von Furstenberg, Max Mara, Theory, and Cynthia Vincent; Three Dots tees; skinny, dark J Brand jeans; rubber Hunter rain boots; ethereal Lucite jewelry by Alexis Bittar (that's made by hand nearby), Wolford tights, and Cosabella underpinnings. It's a reliable spot for wardrobe basics that aren't all that costly and are both constructed and designed to last, making it a favorite stop for many working women, who are drawn to the store's penchant for clean lines.

145 MONTAGUE STREET . 11201   R: COURT ST; 2/3: CLARK ST   ☎ 718.625.7518
⊕ SHOPTANGONYC.COM

Goose Barnacle

This well-curated men's boutique is fairly new, but its lineage goes back generations to owner David Alperin's Spanish great-grandfather, who moved to the neighborhood in the 1930s, and his grandmother, who subsequently bought and ran the Long Island Bar & Restaurant (now revamped and known as the Long Island Bar) down the street. This authenticity permeates just about everything sold in the shop, which sells Alperin's selection of wearable unisex clothing, footwear, and grooming products, including Malin + Goetz toiletries, housed in two large rotary dial phone booths from the aforementioned bar. About 90 percent of the clientele are guys who live nearby, but Alperin's quest for new and emerging clothing lines, especially from Europe, also attracts buyers from bigger stores to peek at his well-chosen picks.

91 ATLANTIC AVENUE . 11201 🚇 R: COURT ST; 2/3/4/5: BOROUGH HALL ☎ 718.855.2694
🌐 GOOSEBARNACLE.COM

Seaport Flowers

Although skillfully assembled wedding arrangements are arguably its strongpoint, this delightful florist, tucked off Atlantic Avenue, makes even an impromptu weeknight bouquet look worthy of a special occasion. The flowers are extra-fresh and frequently unusual—sourced daily from Europe, South Africa, and New Zealand—with a strong seasonal focus in both color and variety. Also available here is owner Amy Gardella's pick of compatible home items—including, naturally, beautiful vases. Prices are not inexpensive, but longtime fans from the neighborhood and well beyond happily swear by Seaport for its uniformly high quality.

309 HENRY STREET . 11201 ☒ R: COURT ST; 2/3/4/5: BOROUGH HALL ☎ 718.858.6443
🌐 SEAPORTFLOWERS.COM

Home Stories

The color palette at Home Stories is decidedly neutral—white, brown, tan, and various shades of gray—and that's the point: the items in this hardwood-floored, parlor-level space are all about understatement and ease. The clean, intentionally uncluttered expanse has a bit of a European feel, reflective of the tastes of former Switzerland residents and husband-and-wife owners Sophie and Paul Yanacopoulos-Gross, who once ran a similarly minded store in Geneva. But the items here, like oversize sculptural lighting fixtures, crisp bedding, and handmade wooden benches and chairs, have been chosen with the nearby brownstones in mind.

148 MONTAGUE STREET . 11201 🚇 A/C/F/R: JAY ST–METROTECH; R: COURT ST; 2/3/4/5: BOROUGH HALL ☎ 718.855.7575 🌐 HOMESTORIES.COM

Colonie

This inviting restaurant's commitment to using fresh local ingredients is underscored by part of its décor: a wall with about twenty different species of live plants mounted on top, their leaves stretching out above a row of seats directly underneath. There are plenty of delicious greens on the menu—like a crisp sugar snap pea salad over fresh-herb-splattered labne—but there are great choices for meat and fish lovers, too, like a hearty steak with creamy aioli and dark, golden fries, and delicate crab and sharp bottarga mixed into al dente torchietti pasta. The long bar is popular with locals for drinks (like the Cool Hand Cuke, a summer favorite with organic cucumber vodka and mint) and light bites that are designed to share, including specialties like crostini thickly covered with housemade ricotta as well as cheese boards, sourced from acclaimed local purveyor Saxelby Cheesemongers, served with sharp mustard and thin crackers speckled with seeds and baked in the restaurant's kitchen.

127 ATLANTIC AVENUE . 11201 🚇 2/3/4/5: BOROUGH HALL ☎ 718.855.7500
🌐 COLONIENYC.COM

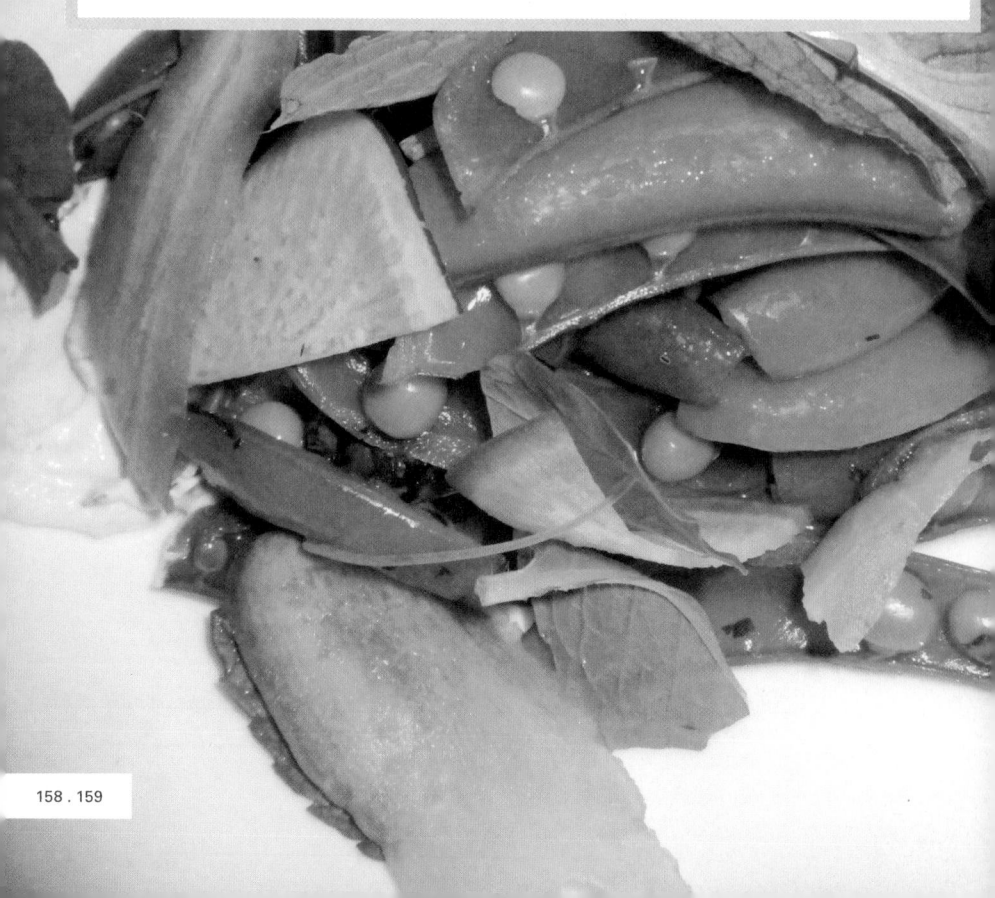

Marissa Alperin Studio

It's hard not to be enamored by this discreet jewelry store, nestled on a tiny street bordered by the Brooklyn-Queens Expressway and across from Adam Yauch Park, a local favorite playground. Alperin creates her very wearable pieces here—you can often find her tinkering with gems and gold wires at a large white worktable inside—with a particular focus on custom-made engagement and commitment rings (which, incidentally, require considerably less turnaround time than most Manhattan-based jewelers). While everything's pretty, the shop's appeal owes much to the personal touch of Alperin herself, whose family photos pepper the store and whose commitment to craftsmanship makes the items here—even simple stud earrings and pendants—feel even more like keepsakes.

25 STATE STREET . 11201 🚇 R: COURT ST; 2/3/4/5: BOROUGH HALL ☎ 718.243.2326

🌐 MARISSAALPERIN.COM

160 . 161

Iris Café

On a quintessentially Brooklyn block, a bit hidden in a knot of cobblestone-paved streets bordered by brownstones, this friendly neighborhood spot looks almost like an artfully styled film set, complete with tin ceilings, dark wood floors, and a welcoming bar in the back. During the day, the food and ambiance is casual, with well-prepared but not overly fussy dishes (housemade granola and yogurt, avocado toast with perfectly runny poached eggs, kale salad). At night, neighbors return for comforting dinners, a concise but well-rounded wine list, and a menu that's a bit more serious (tagliatelle with wild mushrooms, curried cauliflower soup gussied up with mint). Takeout dinner is available as well, and the Iris folks also run a well-stocked gourmet-skewed deli, Willowtown Store #7, a couple doors down the street.

20 COLUMBIA PLACE . 11201 🚇 R: COURT ST; 2/3/4/5: BOROUGH HALL ☎ 718.722.7395
🌐 IRISCAFENYC.COM

Jarontiques

Jarontiques's assortment of home furnishings is idiosyncratic, which is part of its worth-a-special-trip allure. The store is filled with mostly midcentury items, big and small—chairs and tables, art, and also somewhat kitschy Lucite barware, vintage trays designed to serve marzipan and martinis, and hand-carved wooden dough bowls. The array is akin to what you'd find at a well-stocked flea market booth, which makes sense, as the couple also sell their collectible finds at the Brooklyn Flea.

117 ATLANTIC AVENUE . 11201 🚇 R: COURT ST; 2/3/4/5: BOROUGH HALL ☎ 347.463.9894
🌐 JARONTIQUES.COM

Dumbo

A cozy neighborhood, Dumbo (an acronym for Down Under the Manhattan Bridge Overpass), is now an enviable place to live and visit, but it was once a warehouse-filled industrial center that was anything but a residential or welcoming place for a weekend stroll. Over the last thirty years it's been transformed: artists initially moved in, lured in part by those big, then-inexpensive factory spaces, and then, steadily, charming boutiques (like Jacques Torres Chocolate, an early adopter, and Melville House Bookstore), sleek apartment buildings, and young families and their double strollers followed. The current appeal really isn't surprising: Dumbo offers extraordinary views of the Brooklyn Bridge, a thriving art scene (including directional galleries like Smack Mellon), architecture and uneven stone streets that evoke another era, and independent retailers and restaurants that make spending time here a pleasure. It has also, incidentally, become the focal point in New York City of a very modern industry: tech start-ups, many of which are headquartered here.

Brooklyn Roasting Company

There's certainly no shortage of hipster-staffed coffee bars in Brooklyn, with bearded baristas in thick geek glasses pouring lovely patterns into the froth of each cappuccino. The sensibility at Brooklyn Roasting Company's cavernous Dumbo location is the opposite of that: it's a decidedly unpretentious café, decorated with a mishmash of flea market finds, specializing in just one thing: great coffee that's ethically sourced and served up without attitude. In fact, it's become *the* meeting spot in this buzzing neighborhood, whether people choose to gather around the huge glass-topped tables or on its comfortably worn-in sofas. Because this is the company's flagship location (there are a few others, including a much smaller branch at the Navy Yard), the coffee is roasted on the premises, periodically infusing the space with a wonderful, rich aroma. Beans to take home are also for sale, as well as light food and a few branded souvenirs like mugs and tees.

25 JAY STREET . 11201 🚇 F: YORK ST ☎ 718.855.1000
🌐 BROOKLYNROASTING.COM

Vinegar Hill House

There's a serenity about Vinegar Hill House that echoes its immediate surroundings: an enclave of nineteenth-century buildings on cobblestone streets that make you easily forget you're in twenty-first-century New York City, a few blocks from Dumbo's main commercial stretch. The menu is well thought out but also relaxed, offering mostly dishes that sound simple (eggs Benedict and burgers at weekend brunch, extra-tender pork chops and chicken that are wood-roasted in a cast-iron skillet) but are tweaked with additions like tiny house-pickled blueberries or chestnut-imbued béchamel sauce. The décor (wooden tables that look like flea market buys and intentionally mismatched vintage silverware) makes it particularly cozy when it's cold out, but the lightbulb-strewn garden in the back houses the tables of choice in the summer.

72 HUDSON AVENUE . 11201 🚇 F:YORK ST ☎ 718.522.1018

🌐 VINEGARHILLHOUSE.COM

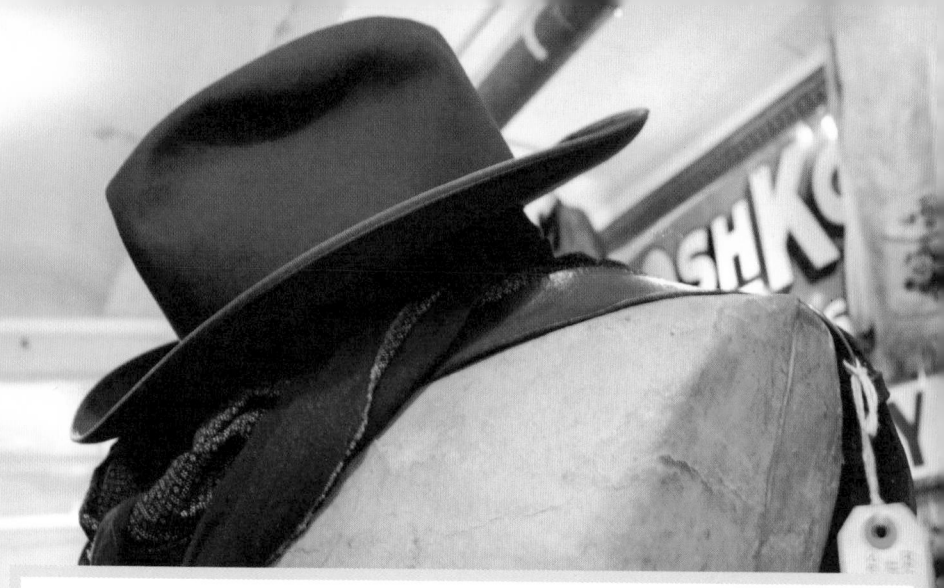

Front General Store

As you'd imagine from its name, there's a little bit of everything at this cavernous retail depot, although the specialty is superbly maintained vintage clothing and accessories, including a vast assortment of unisex sunglasses. There are offerings for men and women, but menswear is a particular strongpoint: you'll find decades-old structured wool felt hats by Stetson and by Borsalino, ornately detailed leather brogues, and vintage military surplus jackets that somehow are neither feathered nor frayed. It takes ample time to look through everything, but it's well worth it.

143 FRONT STREET . 11201 🚇 F: YORK ST ☎ 347.693.5328
🌐 TWITTER.COM/FRONTGENERAL_S

Zoë

This expansive store offers the sort of designer selection you'd expect to find in a Manhattan department store: Saint Laurent crossbody handbags, dresses and jackets from the likes of Lanvin, Alexander Wang, and Proenza Schouler, and a particularly sharp selection of footwear from brands like Jimmy Choo and Valentino. It's a place to find "it" pieces before they become clichés—this was, for example, where many women bought their first Céline bag a few years ago—in an environment that doesn't pressure you to buy. Although the clientele is mostly women who live nearby—from fashion-industry executives to full-time moms—Zoë is also a destination for savvy shoppers from elsewhere in New York City.

68 WASHINGTON STREET . 11201 ☐ F: YORK ST ☎ 718.237.4002
⊕ SHOPZOEONLINE.COM

Shinola

With the opening of Empire Stores—a massive former coffee warehouse on the waterfront that, after being shuttered for decades, has been reimagined as a stylish hotbed of restaurants, shops, and offices—has come the Brooklyn outpost of Shinola, whose robust, guy-friendly, vintage-inspired products are a seamless fit in the neighborhood. The store's décor appears indigenous as well, with the exposed wood and industrial details that are prevalent in buildings here. And at five thousand square feet, the brand has plenty of space to display its unmistakable wares: hand-assembled watches, soft leather basketballs and baseball mitts, sustainably made pocket-size notebooks covered in dark green and navy linen, and even steel bicycles for men and women—all made in America. Shinola's lined-up neighbors in the worth-visiting building include a massive food hall, an outpost of West Elm (founded and still headquartered in Dumbo), and an Italian restaurant overseen by the chic members' club Soho House.

141A FRONT STREET . 11201 🚇 F:YORK ST ☎ 718.875.1204

🌐 SHINOLA.COM

Half Pint Citizens

As it's gentrified, Dumbo has attracted a concentration of young families, many of whom have come to rely on this busy corner store that stocks a bit of everything parents need for their resident mini-mes. There are the requisite adorable clothes—Appaman sweatshirts and soft striped onesies by Under the Nile, plus a choice of pieces logoed with the word "Brooklyn." There's essential gear—UPPAbaby strollers, aden + anais animal-printed crib sheets, hooded towels for bath time, and bibs—as well as toys and a nice selection of books. Baby goods dominate, but there are also many items—like kick scooters—for kids who are a bit older.

55 WASHINGTON STREET . 11201 🚇 A/C: HIGH ST; F: YORK ST ☎ 718.875.4007

🌐 HALFPINTCITIZENS.COM

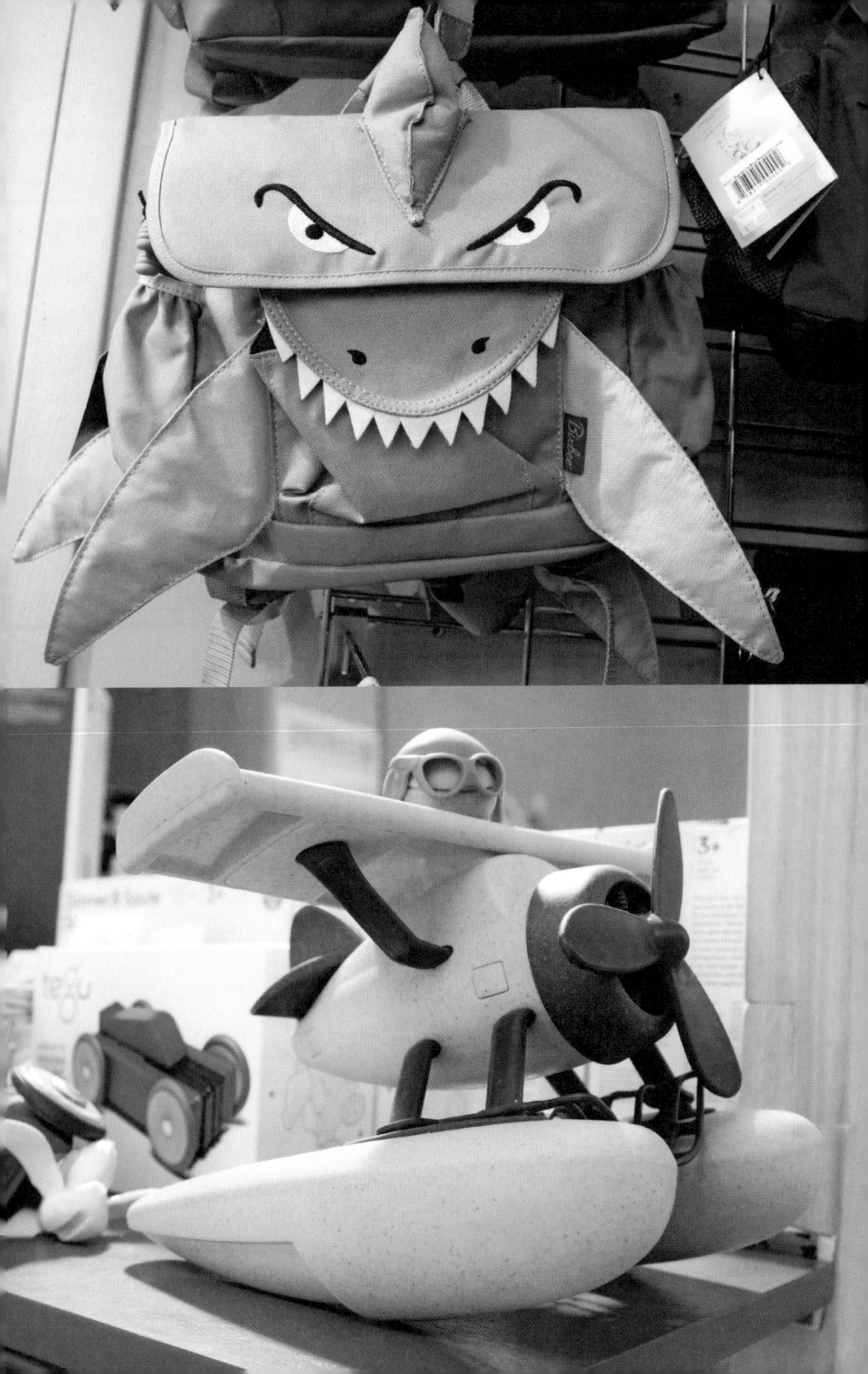

TELEPHONE

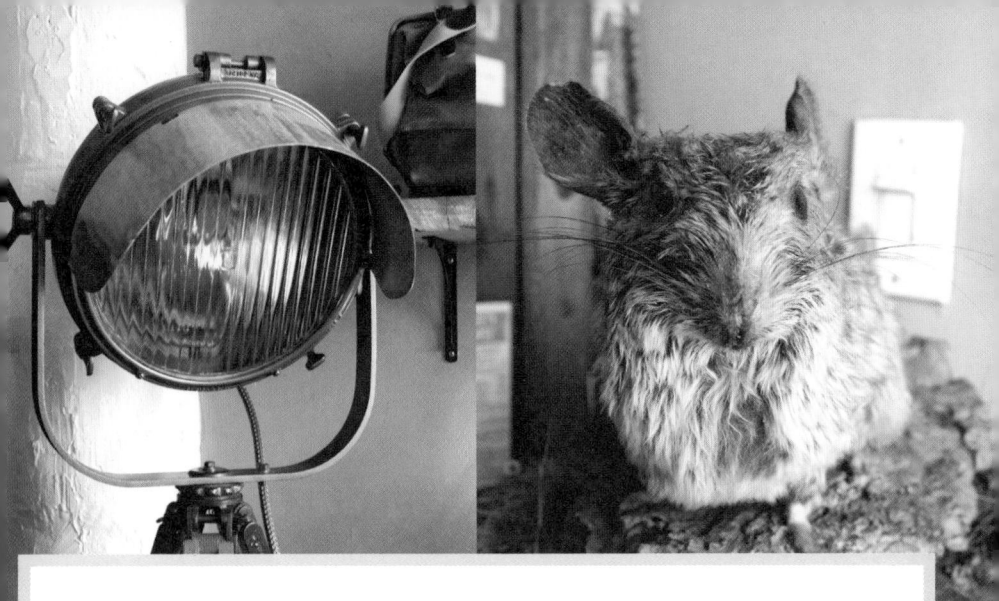

Modern Anthology

With a range of vintage urban artifacts, from a yellow cab's rooftop light to a taxidermied rodent, the décor of this men's clothing and home goods store is the perfect counterfoil to its well-edited stock. The atmosphere is fashionable and a bit clubby, but the selection of the hardy but polished pieces is accessible in both style and scope and includes Universal Works utilitarian jackets, Save Khaki shirts, and Billykirk duffels and totes. Grooming products are also a strength, including skinny tubes of Beardbrand's mustache wax and D.S. & Durga's sophisticated fragrances, conceived and formulated nearby.

68 JAY STREET . 11201 🚇 F: YORK ST ☎ 718.522.3020
🌐 MODERNANTHOLOGY.COM

LIVE, WORK, CREATE.

Park Slope

In the eyes of many New Yorkers, Park Slope is Brooklyn's most desirable community: a perfect blend of tree-lined streets, large old houses and numerous landmark buildings with beautiful architectural flourishes and hardwood floors, a central location, and glorious Prospect Park as its border. Affluent and residential by tradition, the neighborhood has a snug, somewhat laid-back feel—some might describe it as a touch suburban—comparable to an enclave like Cambridge, Massachusetts, or Santa Monica, California. Living here is a mix of young families, executives in creative fields, and a smattering of acclaimed actors (Steve Buscemi and John Turturro) and authors (Paul Auster, Kathryn Harrison, and Jonathan Safran Foer). Unpretentious and calm, the community can feel a little insular, although business owners at local favorites—such as Convivium Osteria, a Fifth Avenue mainstay that you'd swear was in a little Italian village, or Clay Pot Brooklyn, an appealing gift boutique and neighborhood institution known for its artful jewelry—go out of their way to make you feel welcome from the first visit.

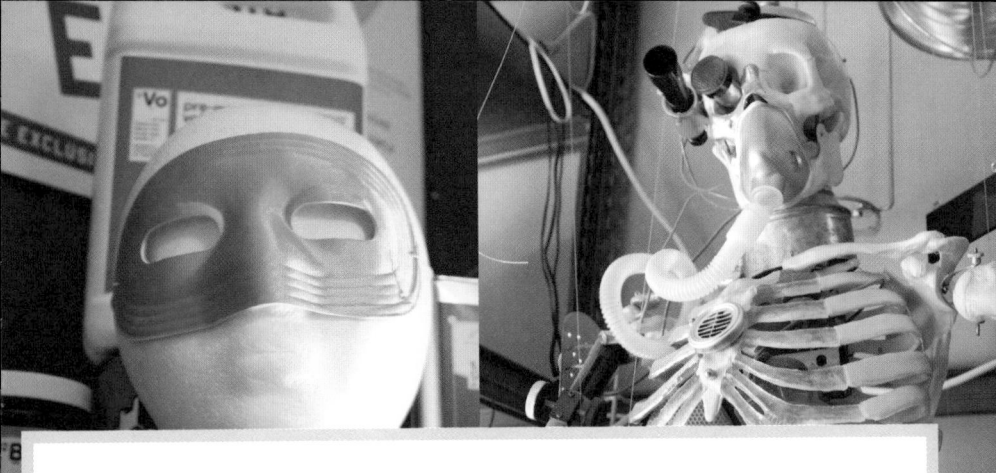

Brooklyn Superhero Supply Company

This highly unusual store that prides itself on supplying the essentials—and nonessentials—related to crime fighting and espionage makes shoppers feel like they're walking into the cheesy ads in the back of a 1950s pulp magazine. The place is filled with kitschy pseudo-survivalist items like secret identity kits, X-ray-vision gear, cans of Magnetism, and buckets of Omnipotence, as well as mugs, books, tees, and naturally, superhero costumes and gear. As fun and spirited as all this may be, the shop is dedicated to community service. Behind a back shelf that moves, not unlike the entrance to a secret passageway straight out of an old movie, is a tutoring center for the neighborhood's school-age kids, which offers help at no charge, thanks to 826NYC, a nonprofit organization that is funded in part by the store's sales.

372 FIFTH AVENUE . 11215 🚇 F/G/R: 4TH AVE–9TH ST ☎ 718.499.9884
🌐 SUPERHEROSUPPLIES.COM

Homebody

There's both sass and class at this diversely stocked South Slope boutique, making it an excellent place to find unique, not-too-pricey presents for just about anyone. There are pretty drinking glasses that would make an appropriate hostess gift for even the most buttoned-up dinner party as well as whimsical, conversation-starting mugs, and candles sculpted in unexpected shapes such as hand grenades, guns, skulls, and animals. There's a nice selection of dramatic silver jewelry (statement rings are a strongpoint) and trinkets with an insouciant, wiseass attitude (makeup cases adorned with slogans like "WTF") that are hard not to smile at. The shop also sells a range of Brooklyn-themed items, along with well-selected, clever greeting cards, often with artwork by locals.

449 SEVENTH AVENUE . 11215 🚇 F/G: 7TH AVE ☎ 718.369.8980
🌐 HOMEBODYBOUTIQUE.COM

The Chocolate Room

This unaffected café is where Park Slope's resident chocoholics come for their regular fix, either to take home or to linger over at one of a long stretch of tables. There's an extensive list of indulgences worth trying, including extra-light chocolate mousse cake, ice cream churned on-site with Sumatran coffee and fresh strawberries, and deeply flavored, rich fondue of melted Belgian chocolate that's served with freshly made graham crackers and marshmallows. The drinks are equally impressive, with multiple takes on hot chocolate, lattes suffused with housemade caramel sauce, and several chocolate stouts, too. It's open quite late by neighborhood standards—until 11 P.M. most nights—making it an ideal spot for a post-dinner sweet fix. There's a second branch at 269 Court Street in Carroll Gardens.

51 FIFTH AVENUE . 11217 🚇 B/D/N/Q/R/2/3/4/5: ATLANTIC AVE–BARCLAYS CTR; 2/3: BERGEN ST
☎ 718.783.2900 🌐 THECHOCOLATEROOMBROOKLYN.COM

V Curated

More reminiscent of a boutique you'd find on the main street of an affluent suburb than a few blocks away from the Barclays Center, V Curated's clothing selection isn't cutting-edge or label-driven, but it's unique and stylish nonetheless. Owner Vanessa Vallarino hunts for emerging American designers from all over the country, carrying a wearable selection of their creations, along with pieces like fluid, brightly patterned dresses she crafts in an atelier downstairs. The shop carries only about ten labels at once, so the clothing is a focused curation rather than a mishmash of styles. There's also a smattering of jewelry and quite a few men's items as well.

456 BERGEN STREET . 11217 🚇 B/Q: 7TH AVE; 2/3: BERGEN ST ☎ 347.987.4226
🌐 VCURATED.COM

Annie's Blue Ribbon General Store

Annie's carries a varying magnitude of items that are too tempting to pass up, so much so that you'll convince yourself that you truly need them, like a coffee mug with a ceramic animal sitting inside at the bottom or a box of six press-on fake mustaches for yourself or your dog. But that's why this is such a great place for gifts—there are plenty of options for even recipients that seem to have everything. There are also good-looking takes on a few bona fide essentials, like bright pink staplers; trim, boldly patterned BPA-free refillable water bottles; and gadgets to help perfect both morning cups of joe and dinner party margaritas. Given its location in family-friendly Park Slope, the shop offers toys and baby-related items (a rattle shaped like a MetroCard, for example), and the store sometimes gets crowded with the stroller set, but the unflappable staff is always helpful and smiling.

232 FIFTH AVENUE . 11215 🚇 R: UNION ST ☎ 718.522.9848
🌐 BLUERIBBONGENERALSTORE.NET

Talde

On a corner where you might expect to find a beer-on-tap bar or burger-centric bistro, this buzzing, continually packed restaurant offers genuinely inventive Asian dishes: just-greasy-enough pretzel-flavored dumplings filled with pork and served with addictive sesame oil–laced mustard, fried rice speckled with flakes of king crab and crimson bits of chunky tobiko, or tiny globs of citrusy guacamole on top of chunky rectangles of sushi rice. It usually takes a while to get a table at this no-reservations spot, but the dark mahogany bar—with its long list of affordable, weeknight-dinner-appropriate wines—is an absolutely pleasurable place to wait.

369 SEVENTH AVENUE . 11215 🚇 F/G: 7TH AVE ☎ 347.916.0031
🌐 TALDEBROOKLYN.COM

A. Cheng

The women's clothing and accessories at this unassuming boutique prioritize a practical sense of functionality without ever sacrificing unquestionable, if nonchalant, style. The shop offers an uncomplicated collection of pieces designed in-house by owner Alice Cheng—loosely cut fluid dresses, for example, in bright red silk and printed nubby linen, that could work in an office or with flip-flops—as well as selections from other lines, like Ace & Jig and Objects Without Meaning. There are also shoes by Soludos and Maryam Nassir Zadeh, crisp Swedish raincoats by Stutterheim, quietly in-vogue golden necklaces and earrings, and breezy bags and clutches. Although there's a seasonal feel to the merchandise, the focus is on pieces to wear for years instead of just during a passing, on-trend moment.

466 BERGEN STREET . 11217 🚇 B/Q: 7TH AVE; 2/3: BERGEN ST ☎ 718.783.2826
🌐 ACHENGSHOP.COM

HOLLA

Items of Interest

This reliable source of decorative gifts and small home beautifiers offers a wide selection that includes Turkish-made throw pillows, brightly colored vases, tea towels, and tableware as well as design books to smarten up even the most weathered coffee table. The shop also carries larger furniture, like long sofas and end tables. The highly browsable space is also the headquarters of DesignCorp, owner Susie Kurkowski's interior design business that has perfected the décor of many of the brick brownstones nearby.

60 FIFTH AVENUE . 11237 🚇 B/D/N/Q/R/2/3/4/5: ATLANTIC AVE–BARCLAYS CTR ☎ 718.404.9185
🌐 ITEMSOFINTEREST.COM

Gowanus

The Gowanus Canal, for which this burgeoning neighborhood was named, was once a busy passageway to transport goods manufactured in New York City. That body of water is still a pillar of the area, although it's not the thoroughfare it once was a couple hundred years ago, and is quite polluted. Today, the area is an unusual but appealing modern mix of idiosyncratic small businesses that are destinations in themselves and large industrial buildings, some of which are now used as artists' studio spaces. Because it's near both Carroll Gardens and Park Slope, and rents are markedly cheaper than in those neighborhoods, more families have moved to the area over the past several years. While Gowanus now includes a recent landmark that is perhaps the undeniable proof of gentrification—a huge Whole Foods Market on Third Avenue, which is essentially the area's Main Street—it still has a strikingly grounded, unaffected vibe.

Morbid Anatomy Museum

Even the most blasé New Yorker has to admit that the Morbid Anatomy Museum—a solid black-painted brick building housing a shop, café, and exhibit spaces—is unquestionably unique. Inside are all sorts of gruesome items—a bright yellow two-headed chick preserved in formaldehyde, rubber models of faces infected with syphilis for sale—that somehow maintain a sense of off-kilter, freak-show-esque fun as opposed to the macabre. In the evening, there are lectures and classes—and some are not for the faint of heart—like taxidermy workshops. The museum is an unexpectedly inviting place to hang out, particularly in the ground-level café run by Carroll Gardens's Black Gold Records that serves up a soundtrack frequently featuring goth-tinged classics by bands like the Cure and the Gun Club.

424-A THIRD AVENUE . 11215 🚇 F/G/R: 4TH AVE–9TH ST ☎ 347.799.1017
🌐 MORBIDANATOMYMUSEUM.ORG

Four & Twenty Blackbirds

Without trying too hard or coming off as hokey, this homey café feels like an unpretentious family dining room in a rustic house in the Midwest. That sensibility comes from its co-owners—Melissa Elsen and Emily Elsen, sisters from a small town in South Dakota—as does the main attraction here: pie, or, more accurately, delightfully flaky-crusted pie that's made by hand and evokes dessert on Thanksgiving with every bite. On weekends, there's a line out the door for these sweet creations—considered by many to be the best in New York City, and available in distinctive flavors like salted caramel apple and chocolate julep, with mint and bourbon. On weekdays, the room attracts locals with laptops or friends who know that the other baked goods here, like scones and savory breads, are also delicious.

439 THIRD AVENUE . 11215 🚇 F/G/R: 4TH AVE–9TH ST ☎ 718.499.2917
🌐 BIRDSBLACK.COM

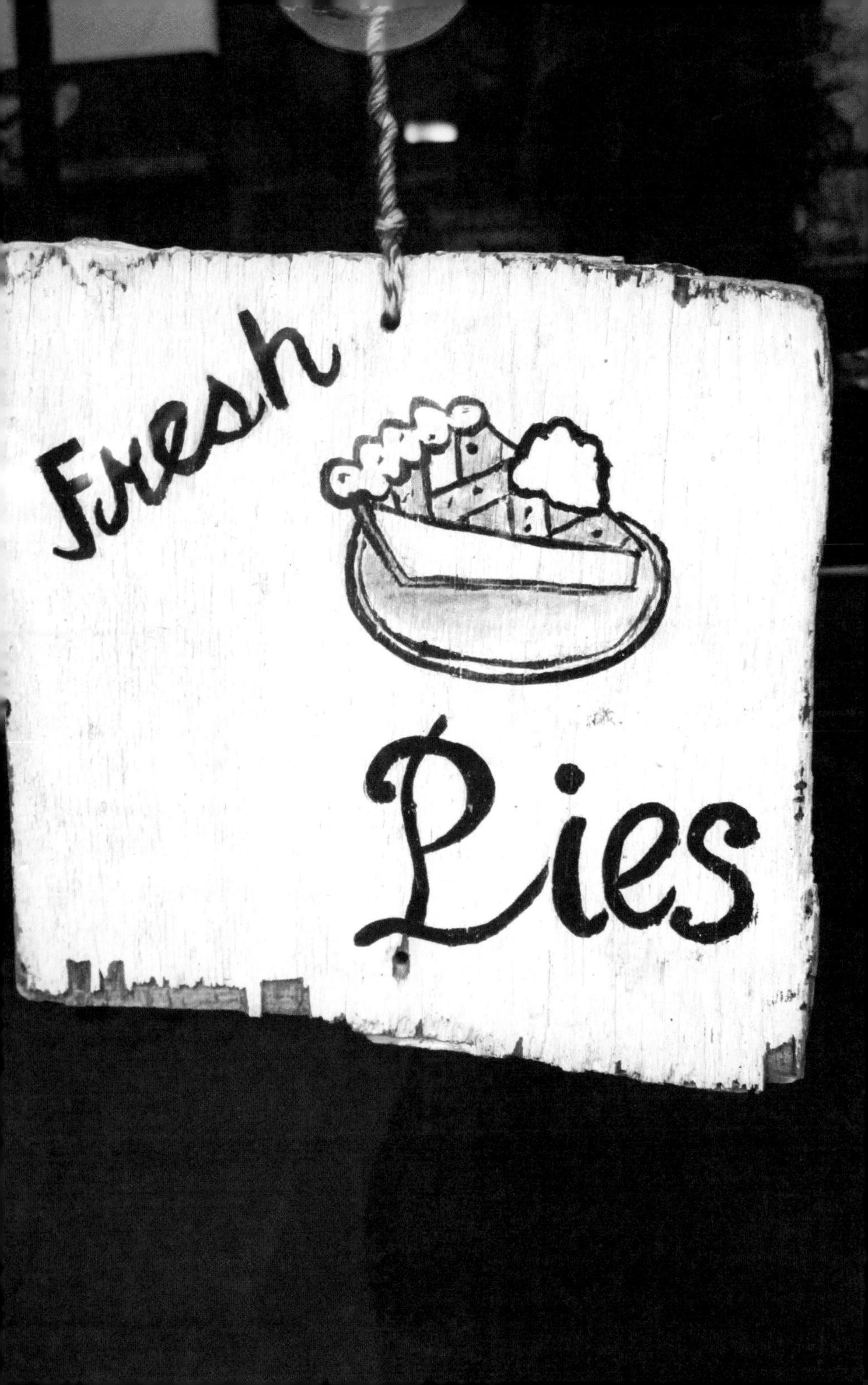
Fresh
Pies

Schone Bride

There's no frilly glitz at designer Rebecca Schoneveld's wedding dress atelier, and that's exactly what down-to-earth brides-to-be from Brooklyn neighborhoods like Park Slope, Carroll Gardens, and Gowanus like so much about shopping here for their big day. Schoneveld's made-to-order creations take their cues from heritage gowns, but her designs aren't too elaborate, although they have plenty of details that make them keepsake-worthy, like layers of French-sourced lace or a line of petite silk-covered buttons running down the back. Schoneveld also offers a selection of dresses by other independent designers, and prices are more affordable—a few thousand dollars less, on average—than at many Manhattan-based bridal retailers. Also appealing is the time it takes to get a dress made: four months, or about half the time you'd need for a similarly customized gown in a grander retail setting.

530 THIRD AVENUE . 11215 🚇 F/G/R: 4TH AVE–9TH ST ☎ 718.788.3849

🌐 SCHONEBRIDE.COM

Walnut Levain
$6

Potato Le
$7

Runner and Stone

This comfortable bakery and restaurant is a Gowanus favorite, as much for the croissants and breads sold to-go on the counter as for the uncomplicated and tasty meals served at the cluster of tables in back. At lunchtime, there is an inventive but casual selection of salads and sandwiches, such as duck pastrami over greens with mustardy dressing and confit pork and cheddar on chewy semolina bread. In the evening the food gets a bit more formal, with fresh pasta that's made in-house and perfectly charred strip steak. Ingredients are seasonal and sourced nearby, and—although dishes veer on the hearty side—regulars always save room for desserts like a brownie sundae with rye whiskey ice cream and caramel sauce.

285 THIRD AVENUE . 11215 🚇 F/G: CARROLL ST; R: UNION ST ☎ 718.576.3360
🌐 RUNNERANDSTONE.COM

Tracy Watts

Up a flight of metal stairs in an anonymous-looking building that was built to produce menswear in the nineteenth century, Tracy Watts' compact studio and showroom might just be the ultimate insider's find for hat lovers. Watts designs beautiful chapeaux for men and women, all made on the premises on antique machines and finished by hand. Her aesthetic is essentially classic with a twist: black fur felt bowler hats feminized with a faux pearl band, wool fedoras that can be turned into a baseball cap with the switch of a brim. Although her creations are sold at swanky stores like Paul Stuart, many customers come in for custom orders, including personalized size tweaks of existing designs. Nothing's cheap, with hats averaging a few hundred dollars each, but the craftsmanship and fabrics involved are aimed to last.

119 8TH STREET . 11215 🚇 F/G/R: 4TH AVE–9TH ST ☎ 718.499.7090
🌐 TRACYWATTS.COM

Cut Brooklyn

Inside a quiet storefront in the heart of Gowanus, Joel Bukiewicz makes just one thing: exquisitely crafted kitchen knives, constructed by hand in a basement workshop with the sort of meticulous details you won't find in typical store-bought cutlery, like specially treated wood handles held together by ornately patterned mosaic pins. The store is open to the public for limited hours every week, selling just a large handful of newly made knives that many customers preselect from photos on Instagram. Equally popular with amateur cooks and professional chefs, Cut offers lifetime care for its sleek culinary tools, which are investment priced and designed to last generations.

431 THIRD AVENUE . 11215 🚇 F/G/R: 4TH AVE–9TH ST ☎ 646.247.9955
🌐 CUTBROOKLYN.COM

Red Hook

Red Hook is bordered by water—namely, the Gowanus Canal, Gowanus Bay, and Buttermilk Channel—and was, for many years, a busy industrial port. These days a great deal of it has been redeveloped, with appealing boutiques and cafés, and new residents moving into renovated, upscale nineteenth-century buildings with character. A couple of retail giants have made their homes here, too—IKEA and the gourmet supermarket Fairway—but, miraculously, neither impedes on the community's small-town feel. The area can get a bit crowded on weekends, when visitors from all over come for a meal, some shopping, and unobstructed views of the Statue of Liberty. Getting to Red Hook is less accessible by public transportation than most Brooklyn neighborhoods—the nearest subway stop is about a twenty-minute walk from the neighborhood's main drag, Van Brunt Street, but it's well worth the trip. There's also a water taxi that leaves from Wall Street's Pier 11 that's a lovely ride if the weather is good, although locals frequently take the public B61 bus, an easy ride from Park Slope or downtown Brooklyn.

Foxy & Winston

There's a whimsical touch to nearly everything in this charmer of a store run by Jane Buck, who has an eye for gifts that are sweet without being too obvious or cloying. Some of what she carries is of her own design, including a range of items, from aprons to baby swaddlers made of vibrantly printed fabrics covered with unexpected motifs, like turquoise blue hedgehogs and deep purple artichokes. The other brands here—John Derian, Brooklyn Candle, Coral & Dusk—all have a handcrafted sensibility. A key focus is also letterpress greeting cards, printed on vintage machinery nearby, often with clever images and sayings. Buck also creates bespoke wedding invitations, a welcome excuse for some customers to happily work closely with her and her sidekick, a friendly beagle named Miss Hope who is the unofficial neighborhood mascot.

392 VAN BRUNT STREET . 11231 🚇 F/G: SMITH–9TH STS ☎ 718.928.4855
🌐 FOXYANDWINSTON.COM

Fort Defiance

Fort Defiance appears to be a simple neighborhood café, but what makes it a standout and a community favorite is the menu, which updates comfort dishes to transform them into something that leans toward gourmet, and its use of fresh ingredients, which come from some of the best local purveyors. During the day, dishes include steel-cut oatmeal swirled with spiced yogurt and grilled cheddar cheese sandwiches with caramelized onions; in the evening, there's asparagus with red mullet bottarga and tender dorade over hearty chickpea tagine. It's also a snug spot for evening cocktails that similarly riff on classics like manhattans and whiskey sours. Ever-present—and essential, if you ask many regulars—is the perfectly charred burger, served on a brioche bun with a side of roasted potatoes instead of the usual French fries.

365 VAN BRUNT STREET . 11231 🚇 F/G: SMITH–9TH STS ☎ 347.453.6672

🌐 FORTDEFIANCEBROOKLYN.COM

Wooden Sleepers

In a space that feels more like a rustic old lodge at a summer camp in the mountains than a boutique that's walking distance from a clear view of the Statue of Liberty, Wooden Sleepers curates midcentury vintage men's clothing with handpicked precision, finding the best pieces culled from insider sources. The evocative pieces are casual but crisp: hefty cotton khakis, dark denim jeans, perfectly worn-in Barbour Jackets. Unlike the clothing mere mortals often find at a flea market, everything is in excellent condition, sometimes refurbished by owner Brian Davis to make them appealing to even those guys who could never imagine wearing something that's been pre-owned. Open only on weekends or by appointment, Wooden Sleepers is a destination store for dapper men from Manhattan and abroad.

416 VAN BRUNT STREET . 11231　F/G: SMITH–9TH STS　☎ 718.643.0802
🌐 WOODEN-SLEEPERS.COM

Baked

This popular bakery specializes in classics with a twist, like Nutella-infused muffins and oatmeal cookies oomphed up with coconut and white chocolate. Nonetheless, the most delectable items on the menu are Baked inventions, like the Brookster, essentially the love child of a brownie and chocolate chip cookie. There's also a Manhattan location in Tribeca, but this original spot, which is mobbed on weekends, has a quiet charm that's hard not love—much like its sweet offerings and, additionally, the yummy sandwiches, salads, and quiches it serves at lunchtime.

359 VAN BRUNT STREET . 11231 🚇 F/G: SMITH–9TH STS ☎ 718.222.0345
🌐 BAKEDNYC.COM

Erie Basin

Although it's huddled among a handful of small businesses in Red Hook, this store would fit in effortlessly in Manhattan's West Village, in London's Notting Hill, or on a narrow Parisian street. The specialty is expertly curated jewelry, mostly antique, with some new vintage-inspired pieces on offer as well. Erie Basin's cross-section of those items is surprising, but it works: art deco diamond-studded platinum bands are juxtaposed with Masonic jewelry, while detailed gold brooches from the 1800s and delicate Georgian diamond drop earrings sit beside more contemporary pieces. The impeccable quality makes this a popular place for couples looking for unique engagement and wedding rings. Also for sale is a concise selection of wonderful vintage furniture, selected, as is the jewelry, by owner Russell Whitmore.

388 VAN BRUNT STREET . 11231 🚇 F/G: SMITH–9TH STS ☎ 718.554.6147
🌐 ERIEBASIN.COM

Brooklyn Collective

Clothing designer Tessa Williams oversees this shared sales space in an appealing little area called the Columbia Waterfront District that's adjacent to Red Hook. At any one time, up to forty creative types—jewelers, painters, t-shirt designers, and pillow makers—sell their wares here, with the lineup rotating a few times annually. Although there's a diverse set of sensibilities and skills on display, the overall aesthetic leans toward the slightly idiosyncratic, like Gamin's weighty engraved bracelets and In the Seam's bold ornamental pillows of iconic New York images. Most of what's offered is quite affordably priced, encouraging shoppers to take a chance on a piece from an up-and-coming designer they probably hadn't heard of when they walked in the door.

212 COLUMBIA STREET . 11231 🚇 F/G: CARROLL ST ☎ 718.596.6231

🌐 BROOKLYNCOLLECTIVE.COM

Kempton & Co.

When British-born Fiona Kempton couldn't find a stylish bag that could discreetly and chicly stow all her gear, she simply designed one—and her brand was born. These days she sells her line of useful totes, clutches, and crossbody bags—all of which are roomy but not too heavy, fairly priced, and made of fabulous materials like silver leather and tactile, weathered, recycled canvas—in a sweet little boutique where she designs and makes them in a small atelier snuggled in back. Also offered are a selection of items from designers who are kindred spirits, including hand-loomed Leigh & Luca scarves and pendants and bangles by K/LLER COLLECTION.

392 VAN BRUNT STREET . 11231 🚇 F/G: SMITH–9TH STS ☎ 718.596.2225
🌐 KEMPTONANDCO.COM

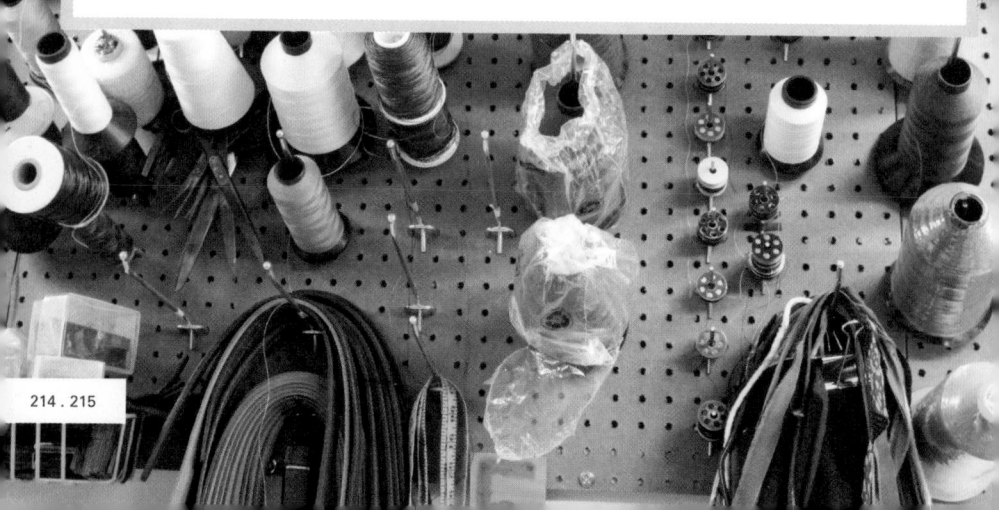

Fort Greene, Clinton Hill, and Prospect Heights

These adjacent communities have no shortage of alluring characteristics: rows of charming residential brownstones; small boutiques and restaurants with personality; cultural pillars like the Brooklyn Academy of Music, Barclays Center, and Pratt Institute. Fort Greene has been home to a substantial African-American community for more than two hundred years, although today it is more of a melting pot, a pronounced mix of new residents and longtime denizens. Clinton Hill, which includes Brooklyn's massive Navy Yard, is a diversely populated community with an expanse of grand former mansions on Clinton Avenue. It's seeing a flood of new homeowners, as is Prospect Heights, with its pleasant nook of nineteenth-century row houses. The latter has a growing restaurant scene on Vanderbilt and Flatbush Avenues, including acclaimed spots like ramen specialist Chuko; Franny's; and old-school favorites like Tom's Restaurant, a classic American diner.

French Garment Cleaners

Don't let the huge vintage sign out front fool you: inside there's a meticulously stocked store filled with understated and uniformly chic clothing, accessories, and gifts for men and women. Housed in a space that was once a dry-cleaning business, French Garment Cleaners favors brands—Isabel Marant Étoile, Santa Maria Novella—with a European lineage; the aesthetic here is less specifically New York Cityesque and more generally cosmopolitan. The shop gets crowded on weekends, with young neighborhood parents walking home from brunch as much as visitors en route to the Brooklyn Flea, but, even then, the unflappable staff is readily available for making suggestions on fit, styles, and new brands of potential interest.

85 LAFAYETTE AVENUE . 11217 🚇 B/D/N/Q/R/2/3/4/5: ATLANTIC AVE–BARCLAYS CTR; C: LAFAYETTE AVE; G: FULTON ST ☎ 718.797.0011 🌐 FRENCHGARMENTCLEANERS.COM

Black Forest Brooklyn

A Bavarian-themed *bierkeller* might not seem like a logical fit in stroller-centric Fort Greene, but Black Forest has an airy and open feel that encourages a plastic-lidded cup of freshly squeezed orange juice or, as the menu calls it, *frisch gepresster orangen saft*, as much as a stein of Hofbräu lager on tap. There's a brunch menu all day, every day—including German items like wurst and schnitzel, along with eggs and pancakes—and a lovely and very popular garden on summer days. Not to miss and ideal for sharing are the homemade Bavarian pretzels, available in two sizes, both served warm and accompanied with hearty, deep yellow mustard for dipping.

733 FULTON STREET . 11217 🚇 B/D/N/Q/R/2/3/4/5: ATLANTIC AVE–BARCLAYS CTR; C: LAFAYETTE AVE; G: FULTON ST ☎ 718.935.0300 🌐 BLACKFORESTBROOKLYN.COM

Thistle & Clover

This compact but well-merchandised boutique is where many of this neighborhood's stylish women come for quick pick-me-up purchases: a brightly patterned sundress, a snazzy scarf, or a just-roomy-enough clutch as the finishing touch on a Saturday night outfit. The slant here is toward new designers, particularly those based locally; in fact, this was one of the first boutiques to carry Mansur Gavriel's it bags. A strongpoint are the earrings, especially the huge selection of precious little studs, some sweet and some sassy, from creative jewelers like Blanca Monros Gomez, Carolyn A'Hearn, Rebecka Froberg, and Sarah Healy.

221 DEKALB AVENUE . 11205 🚇 B/D/N/Q/R/2/3/4/5: ATLANTIC AVE–BARCLAYS CTR; C: LAFAYETTE AVE;
G: FULTON ST ☎ 718.855.5577 ⊕ THISTLECLOVER.COM

Saffron Brooklyn

It's hard to imagine a more central location than Saffron's nook on Hanson Place—a one-minute walk from the Barclays Center, a branch of Target, and loads of subway lines—but Saffron still feels like an insider's secret on a quiet village street. The main focus is flowers—effulgent bouquets, especially for weddings—but there's much more here: sculptural rings with a hidden nugget of sparkly druzy inside, a rotation of art, and other small gifts. The décor is a bit unusual, with a non-functioning vintage soundboard stashed sideways like a giant bookend on the floor, but that adds to the store's earthy charm.

31 HANSON PLACE . 11217 🚇 B/D/N/Q/R/2/3/4/5: ATLANTIC AVE–BARCLAYS CTR ☎ 718.852.6053
🌐 SAFFRON-BROOKLYN.COM

Red Lantern Bicycles

Even New Yorkers whose main experience of riding a bicycle is relegated to weekend morning spin classes have a good reason to frequent Red Lantern: the friendly café tucked inside serves healthy meals (vegan grilled cheese on doughy ciabatta, granola with berries) and coffee that's made from specially roasted Guatemalan beans, best enjoyed with a splash of housemade almond or cashew milk. That's not to dismiss the quality of the bike service here though, which is excellent, attracting customers from all over the borough and Manhattan, too. Red Lantern will tackle anything from standard upkeep to fixing up bruised-and-battered bikes to building new cycles from scratch. There's also an ongoing schedule of events held here, from bike-related offerings like yoga for regular riders to more general gatherings like movie nights.

345 MYRTLE AVENUE . 11205 🚇 G: CLINTON–WASHINGTON AVES ☎ 347.889.5338

🌐 REDLANTERNBICYCLES.COM

O.N.A.

This well-stocked Prospect Heights boutique has saved style-conscious women living nearby a trip to Manhattan or Williamsburg every time they want to pick up a pretty new dress or outfit-finishing accessory. At its core is on-trend clothing with just enough attitude and priced so as not to prohibit a spur-of-the-moment purchase on the way home from work or after brunch at the Vanderbilt, the highly recommended gastropub a couple doors away. Owner Magdalena Jaworska stocks the store with handpicked pieces from collections like Dusen Dusen, Ilana Kohn, and Courtshop, mostly in neutral colors intended to fit in with what's already in shoppers' wardrobes and not make too loud a statement. The accompanying add-ons—chunky ankle boots, nugget stud earrings, streamlined leather crossbody bags—share the same appealing qualities.

543-A VANDERBILT AVENUE . 11238 🚇 B/Q: 7TH AVE; C/G: CLINTON–WASHINGTON AVES;
2/3: GRAND ARMY PLAZA ☎ 718.783.0630 ⊕ ONANYC.COM

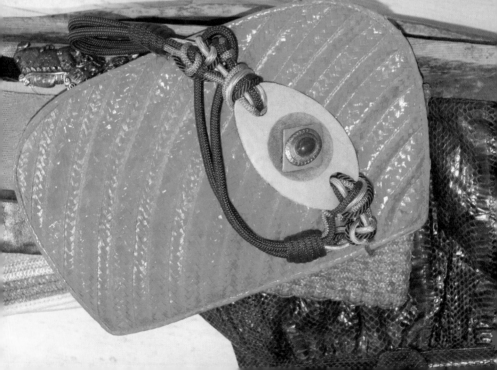

Su'juk

Consider this a one-stop shop for female beautifiers: part clothing boutique and part beauty salon, Su'juk is a place to come for expert hair color and a cute new outfit in one stop. For that last count, Turkish-born founder Su Beyazit offers easily wearable pieces in lovely fabrics, priced reasonably enough to pick up spontaneously for date night, like cute dresses by local designer Samantha Pleet. Also offered here are vintage bric-a-brac and clothing, along with scented candles, soaps, and body oils.

216 GREENE AVENUE . 11238   C: CLINTON–WASHINGTON AVES; G: CLASSON AVE

☎ 347.223.4707   ⊕ SU-JUK.COM

Feliz

This pocket-sized boutique might just be the perfect post-brunch shopping stop, packed with pretty little items that aren't exactly essentials but make wonderful gifts. The selection's quite wide: deep cobalt kantha quilt blankets, ultra-feminine opal necklaces by Lulu Designs, smooth wooden bowls imported from Kenya, and hand-sewn baby toys. Owner Genevieve Platt has an artist's eye, but nothing she sells is too complicated, cerebral, or pricey, making Feliz a neighborhood favorite for more than a decade.

185 DEKALB AVENUE . 11205 ☎ G: CLINTON–WASHINGTON AVES; C: LAFAYETTE AVE
☎ 718.797.1211 ⊕ FELIZBROOKLYN.BLOGSPOT.COM

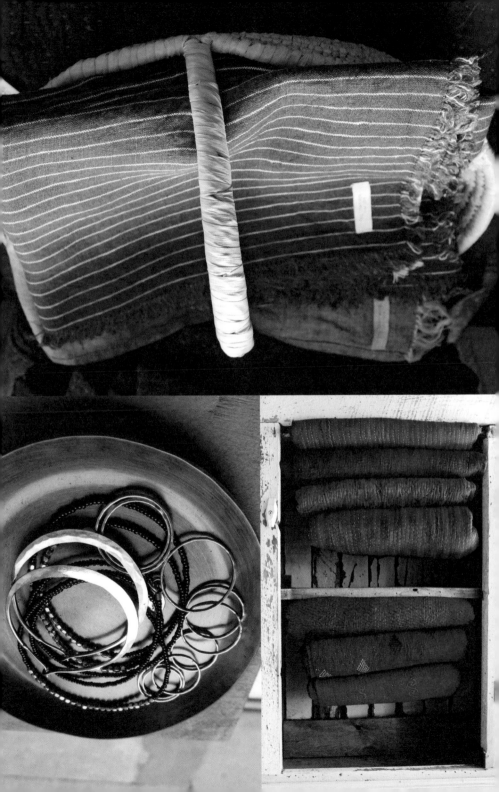

Greenlight Bookstore

This bright bookshop is inviting to readers of all ages, including the neighborhood's many kids, who can often be found perusing the large children's book section categorized by age at the back. There's a wide array of books here, all chosen with the community in mind, so there's a focus on independent presses, design books, and literary fiction. Frequently, there are evening readings, and autographed copies are often available. There are also plenty of giftable items, including decorated notebooks, bookmarks, and greeting cards.

686 FULTON STREET . 11217 🚇 B/D/N/Q/R/2/3/4/5: ATLANTIC AVE–BARCLAYS CTR; C: LAFAYETTE AVE; G: FULTON ST ☎ 718.246.0200 🌐 GREENLIGHTBOOKSTORE.COM

The Finch

If the Finch were in Manhattan, it would most likely be one of those pricey and packed restaurants that require a month's notice and maybe a connection or two to get a reservation after 5:30 P.M. Instead, this extraordinary Michelin-starred restaurant is nestled in a 120-year-old Clinton Hill brownstone, with an atmosphere that is at once vibrant, gutsy, and neither stuffy nor formal and a palpably enthusiastic staff who underline the quality of the food without ever coming across as phony or pushy. And—despite the relaxed atmosphere—that food is major: applewood-smoked squid on top of carrot puree and a pop of shiso leaf, perfectly seared sea scallops accompanied by fresh snails on top of einkorn drenched in grass-green herbs. Chef-owner Gabe McMackin has been preparing food along these general lines for a couple decades at acclaimed restaurants like Blue Hill at Stone Barn and Gramercy Tavern; in his own kitchen, he truly shines.

212 GREENE AVENUE . 11238 🚇 C: CLINTON-WASHINGTON–AVES; G: CLASSON AVE ☎ 718.218.4444
🌐 THEFINCHNYC.COM

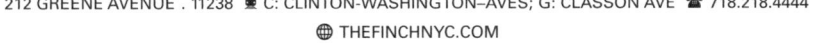

Joya Studio

Joya, a fragrance design studio founded by Frederick Bouchardy, has been producing a beloved line of its own complexly scented items—perfume, incense, and candles—that have been sold at local boutiques for almost a decade. The small company has also created home fragrances for bigger stores like Barneys New York and Harrods and many hotels, as well as what might be the consummate quirky New York City souvenir, a candle that smells like a Katz's Delicatessen chocolate egg cream. Joya now has this stylized retail store on an unassuming street near the Brooklyn Navy Yard, selling its perfumed items and pieces by specially selected compatible brands. In the back of the shop, artisans busily make the candles, with tours offered occasionally so customers can see the process in action.

19 VANDERBILT AVENUE . 11205 🚇 G: CLINTON–WASHINGTON AVES ☎ 718.852.6979
🌐 JOYASTUDIO.COM

Crown Heights and Bedford-Stuyvesant

Not so long ago, these two emerging neighborhoods were anything but genteel: tension, crime, and violence were what most people associated with their streets. But, as in many urban communities, things change, and that's been the case here. Both neighborhoods have seen an influx of new residents, from young families who have been purchasing the ornate townhouses at much lower prices than they'd go for in neighborhoods like Park Slope or Cobble Hill to recent college graduates on a tight budget renting their first apartment. New businesses have come in, too. Some, like Le Paris Dakar, a Senegal-inspired café and crêperie on Nostrand Avenue, have an ethnic flavor that's an inherent characteristic of the area; others, like Lafayette Avenue's Dough, which specializes in inventively flavored doughnuts, have simply found it a successful place in which to headquarter nascent businesses. In spite of its urban sensibility, the area is near Prospect Park and includes wide, tree-lined expanses of Eastern Parkway, so there are tranquil spots of greenery as a counterpoint to the buzzing streets.

Sincerely, Tommy

In a sense, Kai Avent-deLeon, the owner of this attractive store on a gentrifying stretch of Bed-Stuy, is its target customer: a stylish young woman who works in a creative field and is looking for fashionable pieces with panache that she won't see on everyone else. As such, the boutique carries wearable options by young designers, many of whom are local and some of whom offer their work in limited editions. By and large, the aesthetic is mostly based on classic silhouettes with unexpected twists. Also in the mix is a concise selection of bags and jewelry that are on the dramatic side but never overly bold, and priced to make impulse purchases easy. Up front, a pared-down café serves items from acclaimed New York City purveyors like Irving Farm Coffee Roasters and Balthazar, bringing in non-shoppers, too.

343 TOMPKINS AVENUE . 11216 🚇 A/C: NOSTRAND AVE; C: KINGSTON–THROOP AVES; G: BEDFORD–NOSTRAND AVES ☎ 718.484.8484 ⊕ SINCERELYTOMMY.COM

Café Rue Dix

From the outside, this corner café looks like something you'd find in a remote part of Paris, even though it's on a Crown Heights block that might well feel a bit too rough-and-tumble for some diners. Inside, the café serves well-prepared French classics—omelettes, chunky and fresh tuna tartare surrounded by homemade giant potato chips—but the specialties are dishes native to Senegal, where Lamine Diagne, who owns the place with his American wife, Nilea Alexander, was raised. These include a transformative fish stew, called *thiebou jen* that's served over spikes of Senegalese rice deepened with tomato paste, and a traditional chicken dish known as *yassa guninar*. A great deal of the food is on the spicy side—that doesn't stop regulars from asking for a dollop of the hot sauce that's made on premises—but there are less intense choices, too, like pale green hummus. Next door, there's Marché Rue Dix, a boutique filled with an eclectic mix of items sourced from Brooklyn, like vintage clothes and funky jewelry, and from Senegal, like musky incense and Café Touba coffee.

1451 BEDFORD AVENUE . 11216 🚇 2/3/4/5: FRANKLIN AVE ☎ 929.234.2543
🌐 CAFERUEDIX.COM

Little Zelda

This extremely tiny café is nestled on an appealing stretch of Franklin Avenue, near restaurants like Glady's, Pacifico's Fine Foods, and Barboncino. Weekend visitors come for dessert after brunch at one of those popular places; Brooklynites stop by after a run in Prospect Park or for their morning latte. Although the café is in an urban surrounding, there's an unpretentious, almost countrylike ambiance that seems more in sync with that of an old-school coffeehouse on the main street of a small town. In addition to the precisely brewed Toby's Estate coffee, contagiously friendly staff, and charming antique furnishings, the baked goods are a real draw, like gourmet takes on Pop-Tarts (made more sophisticated with ingredients like balsamic vinegar) and sandwiches built around griddled brioche from Boerum Hill's popular bakery Bien Cuit.

728 FRANKLIN AVENUE . 11238 🚇 2/3/4/5: FRANKLIN AVE ☎ 646.320.7347
🌐 LITTLEZELDA.COM

Butter & Scotch

This deliciously dark Crown Heights spot combines two seemingly disparate indulgences: cocktails and desserts. Cupcakes in unusual flavors are a particular specialty, such as gluten-free coffee caramel bourbon, but there are more savory baked goods, too, like biscuits and mustard-enriched cheese balls. There's also truly addictive caramel corn that's additionally sold at New York City retailers like Dean & Deluca. The drink list includes a vodka Collins tweaked with hibiscus and clove as well as alcoholic ice cream floats and milk shakes.

818 FRANKLIN AVENUE . 11215 🚇 2/3/4/5: FRANKLIN AVE ☎ 347.350.8899
🌐 BUTTERANDSCOTCH.COM

peace & RIOT

On the first weekend of every month, this well-edited Bed-Stuy home store fills up with the neighborhood's influx of new tenants: young apartment-dwelling renters and professionals who've moved their families to the area. To appeal to both demographics—plus the mainstays that keep coming back—there are stylish takes on essentials like funky shower curtains and sturdy laundry hampers handcrafted in Senegal as well as hard-to-resist additions, like art deco–inspired birch trays and a selection of cookbooks that's as culturally diverse as the community. Everything's chosen with an interior designer's eye: Achuziem Maha-Sanchez, who co-owns the shop with her husband Lionel, has been decorating stylish homes all over New York City for years.

492 NOSTRAND AVENUE . 11216 🚇 A/C: NOSTRAND AVE ☎ 347.663.6100

🌐 PEACEANDRIOT.COM

Owl & Thistle General Store

There's something for everyone at this multicategory boutique: McClure's pickles and gooseberry achaar by Brooklyn Delhi, sundresses for women and kids inspired by vintagewear, jewelry, fair-trade key chains, and a selection of souveniry gifts with the words "Brooklyn" and/or "Crown Heights." Beyond making the shop a reliable spot for last-minute presents and with plenty to offer in the "spontaneous buy" category, owner Keri Cavanaugh has created a gathering place for the neighborhood's craft-oriented residents, offering classes in knitting, soap making, and, on a neat row of machines tucked in back, sewing for both kids and adults.

833 FRANKLIN AVENUE . 11225 🚇 2/3/4/5: FRANKLIN AVE ☎ 347.722.5836

🌐 OWLANDTHISTLEGENERAL.COM

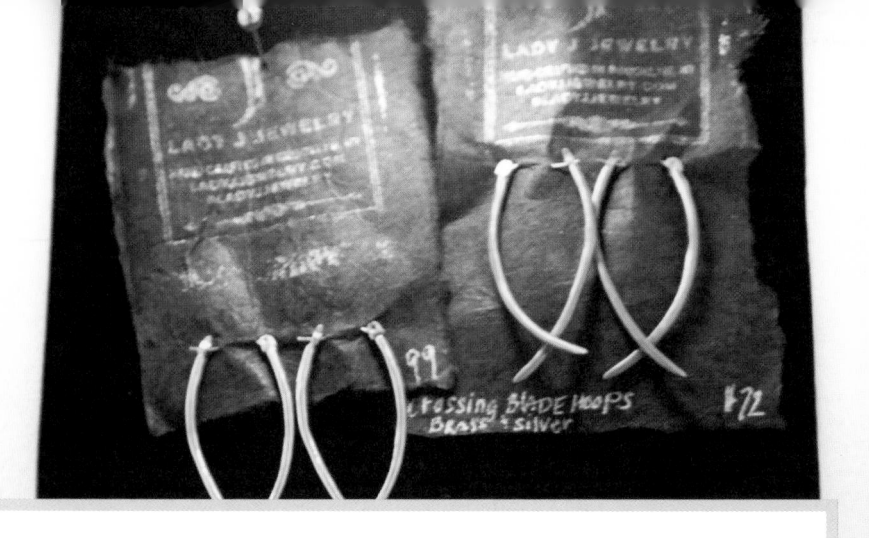

Lady J + 1

This bright store specializes in jewelry designed by its founder, Jessica D'Amico. Her collection, Lady J Jewelry, has a little bit of attitude (pendants with angled metal "twigs," stud earrings with dark stones anchored onto their backs with talonlike golden vermeil claws) and isn't too expensive (most pieces are under $200, even those with semiprecious stones), so it has resonated well with stylish women in this up-and-coming neighborhood. She also carries a smattering of like-minded items: clothes by Brooklyn-based designers Mary Meyer and Samantha Pleet, Apotheke soap, and colorful prints by Fort Greene photographer Anna Campanelli.

675 CLASSON AVENUE . 11238 🚇 2/3/4/5: FRANKLIN AVE ☎ 718.783.0011
🌐 LADYJJEWELRY.COM

Suzette Lavalle

The well-chosen items at this female-centric store have a few commendable qualities in common: they're fashionable, a little unexpected, and less expensive than you'd probably imagine at first glance. With the goal of keeping just about everything under $100, Suzette Lavalle, a stylist who's worked on photo shoots for style-skewed magazines like *Interview* and *Details*, has stocked the store with a large range of items aimed to appeal to the neighborhood, which, in spite of rising rents and more chic restaurants, isn't all that affluent. Included are spunky date-wear separates, pretty folding umbrellas, a bit of jewelry and sunglasses, and colorful graphic pillows that could make even a cheap sofa look chic. The place is so well merchandised that almost everyone who comes in ends up buying something, even if it's just one of the Big Picture Farm goat milk caramels on the counter.

726 FRANKLIN AVENUE . 11238 🚇 2/3/4/5: FRANKLIN AVE ☎ 646.281.4029
🌐 SUZETTELAVALLE.COM

Ditmas Park

This once sleepy community in the borough's Flatbush section is now on the radar of young families and tastemakers, and with good reason: it's friendly, easy to reach on the speedy Q train, and filled with grand Victorian homes that you wouldn't expect to find north of the Mason-Dixon line, let alone smack in the middle of Brooklyn. Many of those homes were built at the beginning of the twentieth century, when the neighborhood first became widely residential, and remain, rather spectacularly, intact. As the area has become more popular, a number of impressive restaurants and shops have opened on or near Cortelyou Road, Ditmas Park's main retail strip, attracting plenty of weekend day-trippers, especially from elsewhere in Brooklyn. Nonetheless, the area still maintains its authentic, communal feel even with that regular influx every Saturday and Sunday.

Sycamore Bar & Flower Shop

Combining a flower shop with a dark-in-the-daytime bar might sound illogical, but somehow it works at this very friendly spot in the heart of Ditmas Park that's popular with weekend visitors and longtime locals alike. When the weather is good, food vendors are regularly invited to set up shop in the large landscaped backyard for an evening. (Try Johnny Lupiani's Awesome BBQ: his dishes pair well with Sycamore's draft beer and American whiskeys.) During colder months, the backyard gets covered and turned into "The Lodge": a heated tent that looks like a suburban basement rec room, complete with a VCR and board games. For all, there are the blossoms, laid out up front; the shop offers beautiful floral bouquets to go and also does special-order arrangements for weddings and other occasions.

1118 CORTELYOU ROAD . 11218 🚇 B/Q: CORTELYOU RD ☎ 347.240.5850

🌐 SYCAMOREBROOKLYN.COM

Collyer's Mansion

This shop's name was inspired by the Collyers, two brothers who gained notoriety in the 1930s and 1940s as hoarders, overfilling their uptown Manhattan home with piles of books, art, furnishings, and assorted other paraphernalia. Although this cheerful boutique doesn't explicitly encourage excess, it does offer plenty of cute home items that are hard to resist, like patterned washcloths from Japan, jade-green drinking glasses, and all sorts of pillows and lighting. It's truly a neighborhood store—with a daily mid-afternoon influx of moms bringing their kids home from school and homeowners who stop by early evening on their way back from work—that's as popular for items purchased to keep as those intended as gifts.

368 STRATFORD ROAD . 11218 🚇 B/Q: CORTELYOU RD ☎ 347.240.2227
🌐 SHOPTHEMANSION.COM

The Farm on Adderley

Weekend brunch is an especially busy meal at this approachable farm-to-table restaurant, where there's usually a handful of people, including a few toddlers in strollers, waiting outside on Saturday and Sunday mornings as the doors are opening. But weekdays here are bustling, too, when regulars come by for uncomplicated dishes made with top-tier ingredients, like light-as-air omelettes with caramelized onions and locally sourced cheddar, a mayo-less Italian tuna salad sandwich, pan-seared striped bass and farro risotto, and a perfectly grilled burger served on top of an English muffin. On warm days, there's a large backyard garden that's ideal for lingering over a slice of almond brown butter cake and a cup of Brooklyn Roasting Company coffee.

1108 CORTELYOU ROAD . 11218   B/Q: CORTELYOU RD ☎ 718.287.3101
🌐 THEFARMONADDERLEY.COM

Sacred Vibes Healing

In a sense, Sacred Vibes is a pharmacy—it just stocks all sorts of teas, tinctures, and essential oils instead of prescription pills, aspirin, and cold medicine. At least that's how customers from all over the area think of this unadorned store, which sometimes has the herbaceous scent of a burning sage stick. People come in for help tackling everything from insomnia to psoriasis to a desire to shed a few pounds. Overseeing it all is earth-mothery store owner Karen Rose, who creates customized herbal regimens as well as the pre-blended treatments on offer.

376 ARGYLE ROAD . 11218 🚇 B/Q: CORTELYOU RD ☎ 718.284.2890
🌐 SACREDVIBESHEALING.COM

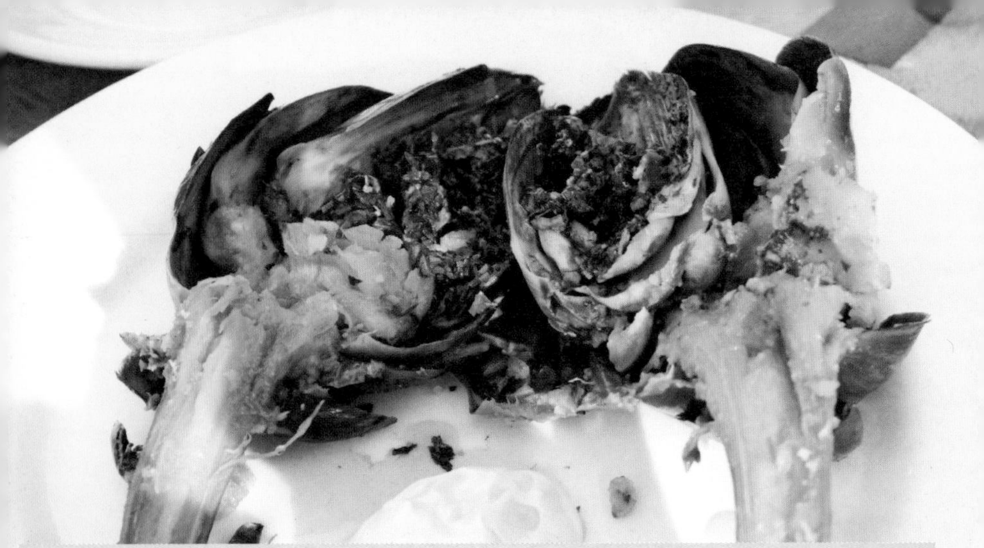

Lea

This affable restaurant is the type of local place you'd go on a weeknight, except the food is good enough to travel for any time, from brunch to dinner. The kitchen's focal point is a neatly tiled, dome-shaped Stefano Ferrara oven—imported from Naples and fired up with wood just about all the time—that also fuels what's arguably the best thing on the menu: thin-crust pizza daubed with broccoli rabe and creamy ricotta or prosciutto, arugula, and mozzarella. But there are other specialties not to miss: giant arborio rice balls stuffed with homemade meat ragu, perfectly sauced pastas, and, during the day, chunky slices of polenta smothered in mild homemade tomato sauce and topped with a pair of sunny-side-up eggs. The restaurant's many loyal regulars know to save room for dessert, namely a slice of pistachio cake baked in that oven.

1022 CORTELYOU ROAD . 11218 🚇 B/Q: CORTELYOU RD ☎ 718.928.7100
🌐 LEABROOKLYN.COM

Farther Afield

At seventy-one square miles, Brooklyn encompasses many communities. This book covers the main neighborhoods, but, of course, there are others, many of which are frequently overlooked, particularly by visitors to New York City. That's a shame, because there's a deep authenticity and charisma to the best of them that makes them well worth a visit and justifies the extra traveling time it takes to get there by subway. Bay Ridge—a longtime Italian neighborhood that has seen a growth in its Muslim population over recent years—is an energetic blue-collar community with especially good restaurants and delis. Bargain lovers will also find a gargantuan branch of the discount department store Century 21, which was founded here. Midwood has a large Jewish population, so relaxed outdoor cafés with kosher dishes are common. An afternoon in Brighton Beach feels a bit like being in a small town in Russia, with Cyrillic signs all around and an endless choice of Eastern European delis. Sunset Park, with its diverse mix of ethnicities, is reestablishing itself as a hotbed of thriving businesses. As is so common in Brooklyn, the sense of pride in these communities is noticeable and, even if you're just there for a few hours, more than slightly infectious.

Tanoreen

Located in the residential neighborhood of Bay Ridge, Tanoreen is an unpretentious restaurant serving such delicious Middle Eastern food that those who aren't local are happy to make the trek. The menu offers many dishes you'd expect—aromatic tabouleh, garlicky hummus, tender lamb shish kebab—and some you might not, like eggplant stuffed with walnuts and sautéed dandelion greens. Not to miss is the *shulbato*, bulgar wheat cooked low-and-slow with tomatoes, red peppers, and spices. Tanoreen is particularly crowded on weekends, so reservations are a must, as is an order of flaky and sweet baklava for dessert.

7523 THIRD AVENUE . 11209   🚇 R: 77TH ST   ☎ 718.748.5600
🌐 TANOREEN.COM

HÔM

There's a lovely spirit of southern hospitality at this community favorite, located, appropriately enough, near the southwestern tip of Brooklyn, deep in Bay Ridge, with a view of the Verrazano–Narrows Bridge down the street. The main attraction here is brunch—served Wednesday through Sunday— and the southern-tinged dishes like eggs Benedict on buttermilk biscuits with rich savory sausage gravy. The place is mobbed on weekends, so make a reservation. There's also a consistently pleasing selection of home items on sale here, like scented candles and pretty mugs, which make it more than just a place for a relaxed meal with friends.

8804 THIRD AVENUE . 11209 ☖ R: 86TH ST ☎ 718.238.4466
🌐 THEHOMSTORE.COM

Circa Vintage House

Circa looks unassuming—a cluttered storefront on a mostly residential Bay Ridge street, without fancy displays or even much organization—but it's where you just might find that Chanel or Gucci bag you've always wanted at a fraction of its original price. Designer-savvy Bay Ridge locals come here to find delicately worn Christian Louboutin shoes and Louis Vuitton totes discounted heavily—and, typically, even more so than on eBay or at other vintage consignment specialists. Nonetheless, what makes this boutique really special is a hodgepodge of cool curios—old statues, vintage tins, and metal brooches and badges—mixed in with the designer pieces. Like most stores of this ilk, the best items sell quickly and stock changes regularly, but if you can't find the Lanvin shoes you're longing for here, the original and enormous branch of New York City's beloved discount retailer Century 21 is just a few blocks away.

276 88TH STREET . 11209 🚇 R: 86TH ST OR BAY RIDGE–95TH ST ☎ 917.674.9631
🌐 NO WEBSITE

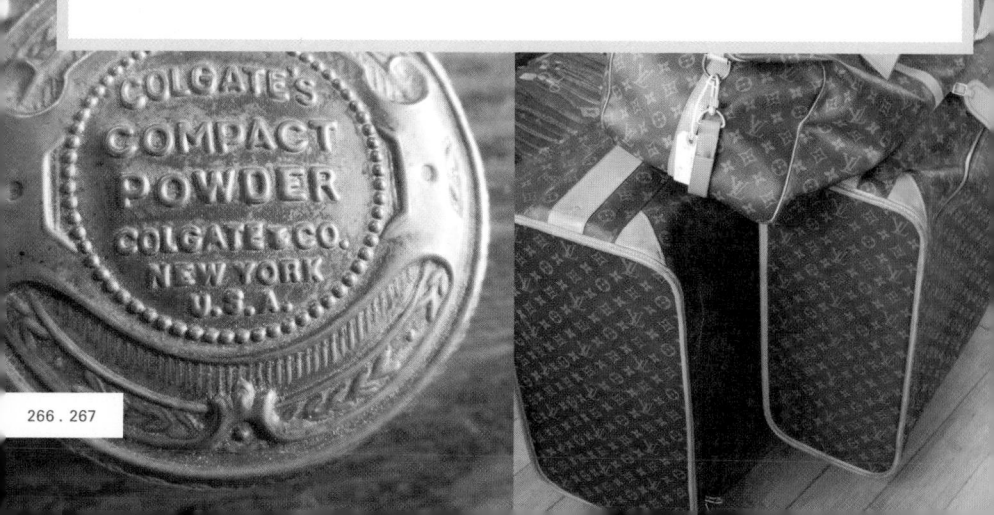

Tatiana Restaurant and Nightclub

Many New Yorkers refer to Brighton Beach—the oceanfront community near Coney Island, deep in Brooklyn but easily reachable via subway—as Little Odessa, due to the large number of Russian immigrants who live and work there. For a literal taste of the neighborhood, diners from all over the city come to Tatiana, a large restaurant on the area's wooden boardwalk that specializes in borscht, chicken kiev, and shish kebabs. With evenings on the boisterous side—there's a live show, dancing, and copious amounts of vodka served—food lovers come at lunchtime to sit at the many outdoor tables for both red and black caviar, salads, and people watching.

3152 BRIGHTON 6TH STREET . 11235 🚇 B/Q: BRIGHTON BEACH ☎ 718.891.5151
🌐 TATIANARESTAURANT.COM/NYC

Chuckie's

For most followers of fashion, designer labels like Marni and Miu Miu bring to mind images of Milan instead of Midwood, the decidedly nontouristy Brooklyn community in which this well-stocked store has been selling top-tier footwear since 1980. Chuckie's has an inarguably deep selection of covetable brands for both men and women, including Gucci, Salvatore Ferragamo, Jimmy Choo, Proenza Schouler, Dior, and Pierre Hardy. Although it's not exactly centrally located and prices are, understandably, on the steep side, the selection attracts shoppers from well beyond the store's immediate radius.

1304 KINGS HIGHWAY . 11229 🚇 B/Q: KINGS HWY ☎ 718.376.1003
🌐 CHUCKIESBROOKLYN.COM

Industry City

Initially conceived in 1895 as an intermodal hub to provide wholesalers in nearby Manhattan with an inexpensive location from which to import, export, and manufacture goods, this gargantuan, buzzing Sunset Park behemoth has seen a renaissance; the six-million-square-foot complex now houses everything from Li-Lac Chocolates' Willy Wonka–style factory to the training center for the Brooklyn Nets basketball team as well as a large branch of furniture retailer Design Within Reach. A key draw for visitors is the Food Hall, an area focused on gourmet food vendors that includes outposts of beloved Brooklyn brands like One Girl Cookies, Blue Marble Ice Cream, and Liddabit Sweets.

274 36TH STREET . 11232 🚇 D/N/R: 36TH ST ☎ 718.965.6450
🌐 INDUSTRYCITY.COM

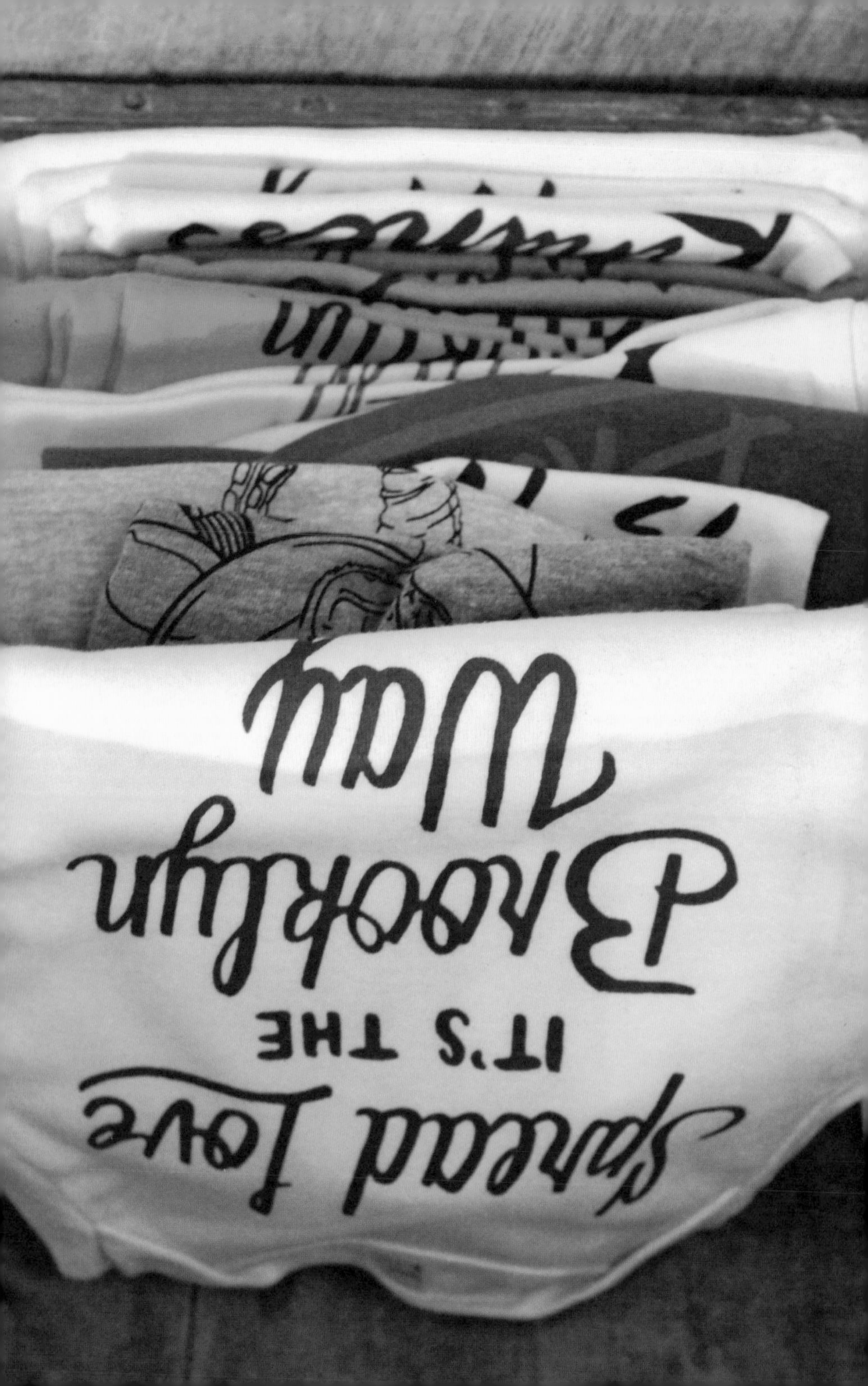
Spread Love
IT'S THE
Brooklyn
Way

MADE
IN
BROOKLYN

Speak
Brooklynese
like a native!

Creamuh

Creamuh

Creamuh

LISTINGS INDEX

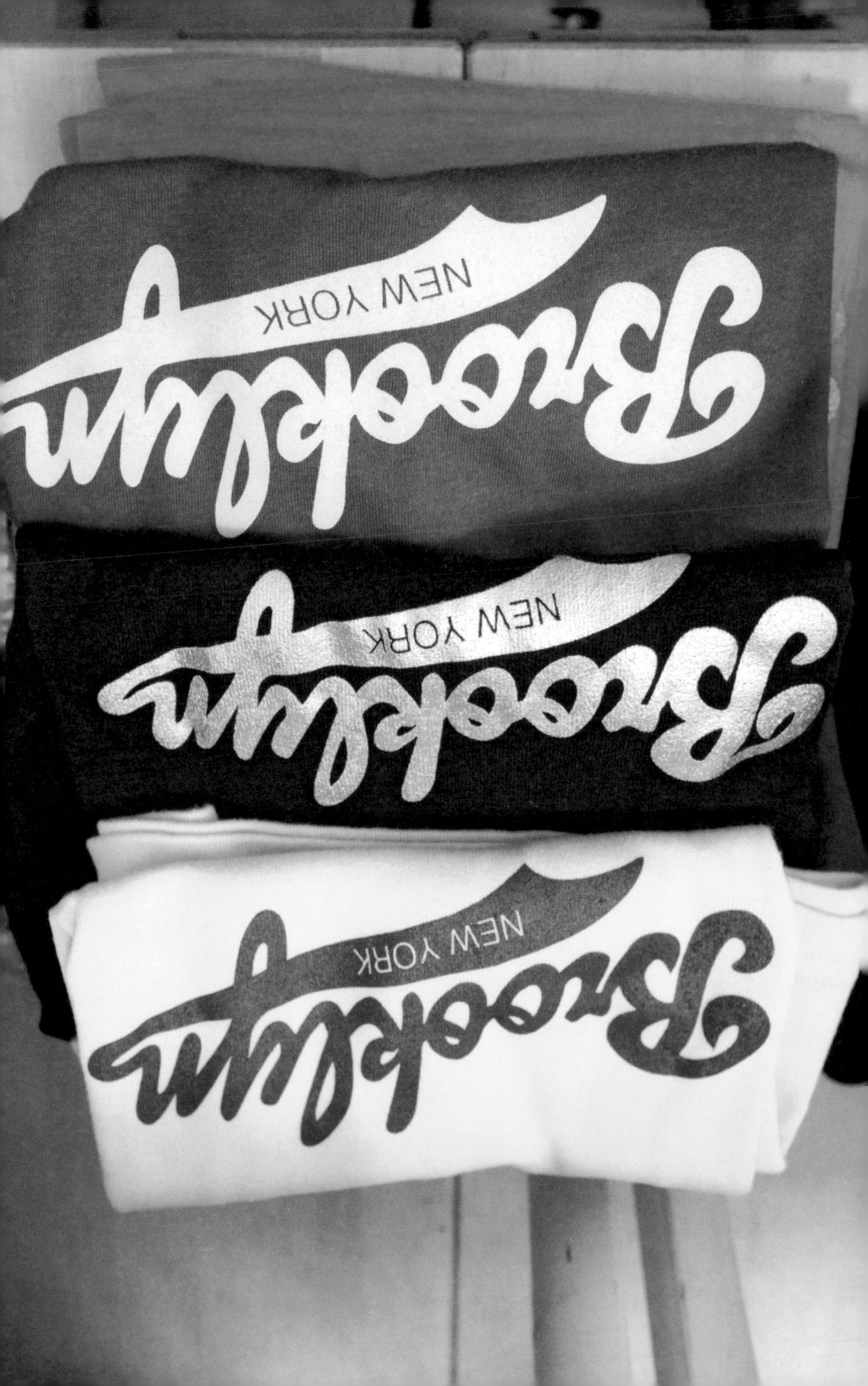

ACKNOWLEDGMENTS

There's an adage that says you should write about what you know. I'll add that it's best to write about a subject you love, are fascinated by, and that you feel so deeply connected to that it's an inherent, immutable part of who you are, like a birthmark or the color of your eyes. That is, quite simply, the way I feel about Brooklyn—and, for that, I have one person to thank: my beloved father, Raoul Lionel Felder, who raised me to be proud of our Brooklyn lineage decades before the area was cool. He also, incidentally, taught me to appreciate the fine details of beautiful things—from hand stitching on jacket cuffs to the notes in fragrance to the right amount of ganache coating on a black-and-white cookie—so, really, I have much to be grateful for.

Huge thanks go to my dynamo editor, Elizabeth Viscott Sullivan, for tapping into that Brooklyn-ness and helping it shine. Her boundless enthusiasm and encouragement have been empowering and as wonderful as cannoli from Fortunato Brothers (which is pretty darn wonderful indeed). I'm also tremendously appreciative for the help of Lynne Yeamans, Niloo Tehranchi, Amy Saidens, and the entire Harper Design team, as well as the support of Marc Beckman and Nancy Chanin at DMA, along with the mighty Richard Grabel.

While working on this book, I've been so very lucky to have a handful of special Brooklyn-based friends who have served as sounding boards, cheerleaders, and marvelous company (and co-eaters) at the borough's best restaurants. Special thanks go out to that crew—Nancy Carlson, Sandra Chiu, Steve Dumain, Katherine Ensslen, and Eden Grimaldi—as well as some non-Brooklynites, too: Kate Holmes and Alan McGee, James Felder, Susan Miller, Parise Sellitti, John Snitzer, and Shelley von Strunckel. My gratitude also goes to the numerous small business owners included in this book for welcoming me into their compelling spaces and sharing their stories, so many of which are truly inspirational.

My goal, of course, is that this book will instill in readers my deep love of New York's most vibrant borough. Working on this project has underlined that affection, for which I'm grateful as well.

HarperCollins books may be purchased for educational,
business, or sales promotional use. For information
please e-mail the Special Markets Department at
SPsales@harpercollins.com.

First published in 2016 by
Harper Design
An Imprint of HarperCollins*Publishers*
195 Broadway
New York, NY 10007
Tel: (212) 207-7000
Fax: (855) 746-6023
www.hc.com
harperdesign@harpercollins.com

Distributed throughout the world by
HarperCollins*Publishers*
195 Broadway
New York, NY 10007

ISBN 978-0-06-239743-0

Library of Congress Control Number: 2014952995

Book design by Niloo Tehranchi
Map illustration by Amy Saidens

Printed in China
First Printing, 2016

ABOUT THE AUTHOR

Rachel Felder is a journalist who writes about travel, trends, and style for a wide range of publications. Her work has appeared in the *New York Times*, *Financial Times*, *Travel and Leisure*, *Departures*, *New York* magazine, *People*, *Rolling Stone*, *Town and Country*, *Women's Wear Daily*, and on the websites of *Vanity Fair* and *The New Yorker*. The author of *Manic Pop Thrill* (Ecco) and coauthor (with Reed Krakoff) of *Fighter* (Viking Studio), she has appeared at conferences like TEDxOxford and SxSW.

Twitter: @rachelfelder; Instagram: @rachelfelder